Backwoods Boy

An Illustrated Memoir of Growing Up in Rural New Brunswick in the Fifties and Sixties

Richard Irving

BACKWOODS BOY copyright © 2023 by Richard Irving

All content contained herein, unless otherwise noted, is copyright © 2023 by Richard Irving.

Photo Credits

Figures 1, 2, 6, 7, 8, 10, 14, 30, 42 from family files, taken by Unknown

Figure 11 taken by Harold Irving

Figure 15 taken by Frank Sauerman

Figures 21, 31 taken by Richard Irving

Cover design by Nino Vecia, NinoVecia.com

Cover sketch of original Irving farmhouse by R. Irving

Author photo by Heather Doyle Images

Copyedit by ScribeCat.ca

All rights reserved. No part of this publication may be reproduced, stored, or transmitted in any manner, electronic, mechanical, photocopying, recording, scanning, or otherwise without written permission by the author (except in the case of brief quotations embodied in critical articles or reviews). Thank you for the support of the author's rights.

For information, contact: Richard Irving, bkwdsby2020@gmail.com

This book is written in Canadian English.

First Edition, First Printing: May 2023

Second Printing: September 2023

Third Printing: December 2024

Printed in Canada by Printing Legacy Inc.

ISBN: 978-1-7389328-1-8 (hardcover)

ISBN: 978-1-7389328-3-2 (trade paperback)

ISBN: 978-1-7389328-2-5 (eBook)

Order at rickwrites.ca

This book is dedicated to my parents, Harold and Gladys Irving, who made me what I am; to my son Alex, my daughter-in-law, Keri; and to my grandsons. Colby, Wyatt, and Lachlan, who give me hope for the future.

I also dedicate the book to all the quiet, unremarkable people who lived the best lives they could. They are typically unsung, unheard, and often forgotten. They are the majority, largely ignored by history and historians. My people are Hobbits, quiet and easily overlooked—this book honours them.

Acknowledgements

While I alone am responsible for the content of this book, particularly any errors or omissions, many people helped me along the way.

The Humber College writing workshop participants and faculty provided the initial encouragement and guidance to get me started on this project. The incomparable Heather W. provided initial editorial and structural guidance, while Carey A. gave me valuable advice on the composition and execution of my sketches. Isobel S. read and commented on an earlier version, as did Annis K. and Sheila C. Two cousins, Garda C. and Philip Mc., gave me helpful background information on our families. The advice provided by Jeffrey L. was, as always, invaluable.

Finally, I must acknowledge the artwork of Nino V. on the cover, the photography of Heather D., and the outstanding work of Ashley L., who did the final edits and guided me through the self-publication process.

Acknowledgement also goes to family and friends who tolerated me going on and on about the project.

Thanks to you all.

List of Illustrations

Chapter 1
> Figure 1: Wedding, Harold Irving and Gladys Green
> Figure 2: Harold Irving, Airforce
> Figure 3: Moncton, Hillsborough, and Baltimore
> Figure 4: Party Line with Crank Telephone
> Figure 5: Map of Baltimore
> Figure 6: Wedding, James Irving and Elisa Steeves
> Figure 7: Sanford (Sandy) and Margaret (Maggie) Irving
> Figure 8: Sandy, Maggie, Bob, Curt, and Harold Irving
> Figure 9: Irving Family Tree
> Figure 10: Margaret, John, Maggie, and Henry Turner
> Figure 11: Gladys, Richard, Maggie, Garda, Bea, and Omer Irving
> Figure 12: Saint John River at Evandale
> Figure 13: The Green Farm at Mistake Cove
> Figure 14: Uncle Ken with Sylvia and Amanda Sauerman
> Figure 15: The Green Sisters: Georgie, Gladys, Elsie, and Muriel

Chapter 2
> Figure 16: The Original Irving Homestead
> Figure 17: The Old Kitchen
> Figure 18: An Aladdin Lamp
> Figure 19: A Mortise and Tenon Joint with Wooden Peg
> Figure 20: Our Old Barn
> Figure 21: Baltimore Church Built by Rev. James Irving

Chapter 3
> Figure 22: Collecting Sap
> Figure 23: Making Maple Syrup Old Style
> Figure 24: Dad's Sugar Camp
> Figure 25: Picking Fiddleheads

Chapter 4
> Figure 26: Taking Down Storm Windows
> Figure 27: Protecting the Garden with an Electric Fence

Chapter 5
> Figure 28: Picking Strawberries
> Figure 29: Blueberry Rake and a Half-Bushel of Berries
> Figure 30: Haying Old Style

Chapter 6
> Figure 31: Camping with the Guys

Chapter 7
> Figure 32: Stealing a Boat to Go Fishing
> Figure 33: Dick, Waiting for Me at the Mailbox

Chapter 8
> Figure 34: Yarding Logs with a Horse
> Figure 35: Cutting Firewood
> Figure 36: Fool Killer
> Figure 37: Sawing Firewood
> Figure 38: Insulating the Foundation with Sawdust
> Figure 39: Fake Deer Eyes on a Tree

Chapter 10
> Figure 40: Breaking Rocks with Dad
> Figure 41: Harold Blake Contemplates Oblivion
> Figure 42: Crossing the Saint John River on the Ice

Chapter 11
> Figure 43: Shovelling Snow
> Figure 44: Bending the Skis
> Figure 45: Moonlight Ski Jump

Chapter 12
> Figure 46: Garage Modified for Living
> Figure 47: New House in Baltimore

Table of Contents

Preface..1

Part 1
    Chapter 1. My World in the Fifties and Sixties....................5
    Chapter 2. The Old Homestead.. 23

Part 2
    Chapter 3. Spring Renewal...39
    Chapter 4. Getting the Farm Ready.......................................49
    Chapter 5. Summer Abundance..61
    Chapter 6. Recreation..77
    Chapter 7. Summer Lessons Learned....................................83
    Chapter 8. Fall Frenzy... 91
    Chapter 9. Going Back to School... 111
    Chapter 10. Fall Stories... 123
    Chapter 11. Winter Recuperation..137

Part 3
    Chapter 12. The Day Our House Burned Down.......................153
    Chapter 13. From Backwoods to Big City................................ 159
    Chapter 14. Reflections... 163

Preface

As I write this in 2021, I wear a digital watch that tracks my movements, heart rate, GPS location, and outside temperature. That watch connects to my smartphone and notifies me when I have messages. My phone, and the tablet on which I write, are connected to the internet—I can find information immediately. Today, from my desk, I can: make video calls worldwide; teach a class of fifty people from my tablet; or take a course from anywhere in the world. I no longer need to travel to boring meetings and can access most services without moving. While attending a Zoom meeting: I can mute my audio and video to make lunch, nap, or read a book…while still 'participating' in the forum.

People in their twenties and younger have never known a world without cell phones and computers…just living their lives to the rhythm of notification chimes. It was not always thus.

Those of us in our fifties and older remember when these things were the stuff of science fiction. If you wanted to know something, you read a book; and you looked up someone's phone number in a phone book, to hang out with your friends, you went to their house.

Seven decades of changes in technology and society have left their mark. Beginning as a backwoods boy: I grew up to eventually obtain a Ph.D. in Management Science from the University of Waterloo and became a Professor at the "Schulich School of Business" at York University in Toronto—researching the effects of new technology on organisations. I have seen a world transformed by technology. In some cases, made better; in others, not so much.

Still...no one pines for the good old days of dentistry.

Seventy years ago, many rural folks (me included) didn't have running water, indoor toilets, electricity, or telephones. In the 1940s, 1950s, and 1960s, we began to see the beginning of changes that led to today's world. I experienced those changes and saw a globe transformed so thoroughly that people from the forties and fifties wouldn't recognize much of how we now live. However, despite lacking our modern-day technological advances, they managed to live full, satisfying lives—and may have even formed stronger social connections than we do today.

Our post-industrial world is terrific...but amid all this capability, we have lost connections to our roots, our family stories, our oral histories. To the communities and the characters who populated them, where everybody knew your name, who your people were and where you lived. To a way of life that shaped how we do many things today. It's a world that is long gone but which should *not* be forgotten.

So, come back there with me, to life as a kid in the backwoods of rural New Brunswick in the fifties and sixties. Back to a time when we lived our lives to the rhythm of the seasons; when we checked the weather by going outdoors; and when we shared information by swapping stories around the kitchen table (or by gathering for an evening with a neighbour or two and a fiddle). You will meet my people; hear our stories; and learn (or reminisce) about what we did, how we did it, and why. I'll share stories of people, places, and events, with sketches and photos that evoke a sense of times past—when we had no online connections, but we were well connected, nonetheless. And just perhaps...*together*, we can make some sense of how we ended up where we are.

Part 1

Chapter 1

My World in the Fifties and Sixties

I exist because of my father's high blood pressure. Harold Irving and Gladys Green married on a hot August day in 1942. In the photo (Figure 1), they look stiff and posed, though, in person, they were typically relaxed and informal. No doubt they were nervous.

Three months later, Dad volunteered for the Royal Canadian Air Force (RCAF) as a tail gunner.[1] The life expectancy of tail gunners in battle was about twenty minutes. Fortunately for him (and me), his blood pressure was too high for the aircrew. Instead, he trained as an instrument mechanic and served in Canada for the duration of the war. In the photo (Figure 2), he looks happy and relieved to spend the war as an instrument mechanic.

Figure 1. Wedding, Harold Irving and Gladys Green

Figure 2. Harold Irving, Airforce

---

[1] "Canada in World War II," *Wikipedia*, last edited March 23rd, 2022, https://en.wikipedia.org/wiki/Canada_in_World_War_II.

Shortly after Father was mustered out of the RCAF in 1946, Mom and Dad decided it was safe to have a kid—not an original decision. I was part of the early wave of the "baby boom." After travelling around Ontario and Quebec during the war, my parents returned to my grandparents' farm in Baltimore, Albert County.

The farm was thirty kilometres south of Moncton and sixteen kilometres from the Village of Hillsborough, New Brunswick (Figure 3). They moved in with my grandmother (Maggie), as my grandfather (Sandy) had died in 1941. The distances aren't great, but poor roads and bad weather meant we were frequently isolated. As the youngest of six children, my father had inherited the farm with the provision that he would care for my grandmother. She lived with us until her death at home in 1960.

I was born in July 1947, two years after World War II ended. That was also a year after ENIAC was created, which was the first successful, high-speed digital computer. In 1947, the transistor was invented, so my whole life has spanned the age of computers.

Transistors led to Univac in 1955, the first *commercial* digital computer.[2] Like many major innovations, this generally went unremarked… but computing ultimately would change the course of our lives (and lead to the world we have today). Those changes took a long time to play out! It took until the mid-1990s for 'most everyone' to be networked and have access to email, at least, in organisations. By 2000, the internet was raging across the globe…and by 2020, we were tightly connected on many levels.

In 1947, India and Pakistan became independent countries; the UN voted to create Israel and the Cold War began. The polio epidemic was a constant threat (sound familiar?), and the public became concerned about nuclear weapons. On January 1, 1947, the Canada Act came into effect, which deemed all British subjects who lived in Canada as Canadian citizens. Up to then, they had all been British citizens. My cousin Garda (born two years earlier than me) could claim dual citizenship. When I was young, that annoyed me for some reason.

---

[2] A transistor or semiconductor is a device for amplifying, controlling, and generating electrical signals. They are deeply embedded in almost everything electronic. "Transistor," *Wikipedia*, last edited April 18th, 2022, https://en.wikipedia.org/wiki/Transistor.

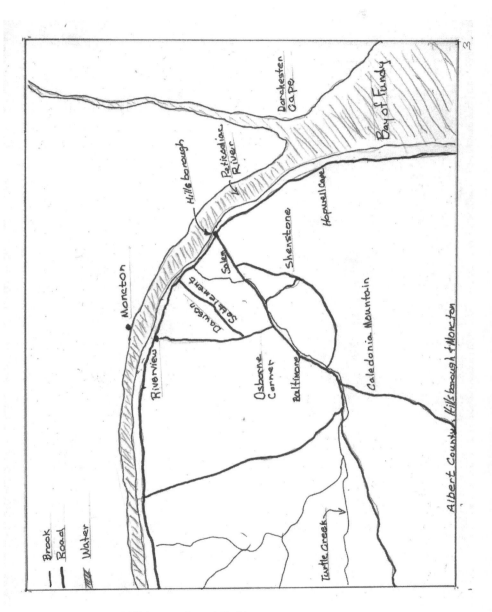

Figure 3. Moncton, Hillsborough, and Baltimore

The post-war Canadian economy was growing; most people had a positive outlook for the future. Sure, they were concerned about communism, polio, and the Cold War; but they had jobs, they could afford a car and a place to live. The future looked rosy!

While Canada experienced a post-war boom, New Brunswick was largely left behind. We had some residual economic benefit from the build-up of the railways and the military during the war, but this dissipated over subsequent years. We returned to lumbering, fishing, farming, and mining. The commodity-based economies of the Maritimes forced many educated young people (including me) to look elsewhere to find employment. Sadly, this is still true today—though that may be changing with Covid-19, remote work, and rising house prices in Ontario.

One of the most significant features of life in the forties, fifties, and sixties was how closely we were tied to the seasons. Part of this was everyday farm life that continues to the present, but it was also due to the technology available...particularly transportation and refrigeration.

Ships, trains, and trucks were the primary method of moving goods. After WWII, we had a sound rail system, but the roads (especially in the Maritimes) were mainly dirt roads—while the few paved roads were not in good repair. Distribution issues kept fresh produce in short supply. We relied heavily on storing, canning, and (later) freezing whatever we produced on the farm...not on supermarkets as we do today.

Because the roads were poor, people travelled less than they do now. Today, the twenty-mile drive from Baltimore to Moncton is a quick trip that might take all of twenty-five minutes. In the fifties and sixties, it was an event that took at least an hour. In terrible weather, it took much longer as we navigated muddy, snowy, or icy roads.

People thought carefully about making a long-distance call because telecommunications were expensive. Today, I have a cell plan with unlimited calling across Canada. And while electricity became widely available in the fifties, it was unreliable in winter—and most everyone planned for power outages. While these still occur today, they are sufficiently infrequent that people are surprised and even outraged. Back then, they were par for the course.

Connecting to the World Outside

For many years, the outside world didn't impinge much on me in tiny Baltimore, New Brunswick. We had a radio and, in the late 1950s, finally got a TV. My parents always listened to CBC News on the radio, as well as music programs and radio plays. *The Moncton Times and Transcript* (a local newspaper) was delivered daily by mail. We had sufficient local and regional news. For a while, we owned a radio that had shortwave channels. I got a thrill out of listening to chatter and programs from around the world. Once, I remember a news broadcast from Australia. I could barely hear it but was enthralled nonetheless.

Most communication was face to face, primarily by just dropping in unannounced. Letter writing was prevalent; and the mail service was quick, reliable, and cheap. We did have a telephone on a "party line." It was an analog phone (no digital phones then) with a handset and a crank. Our number was two short and two long rings. If we heard our ring, we picked it up. A feature of a party line was that anyone else on the same line who heard the phone ring—in our case, the entire population of Baltimore (about twenty people)—could pick it up and listen in if they were so inclined. Some folks had little to do but listen in to most conversations. The benefit was that news passed quickly (if not always accurately) throughout the community.

To place a local call to another Baltimore resident, you just rang the number of short or long rings for the person you wanted. By ring, I mean precisely that. You turned a crank on the side of the phone and rang a bell. If you wished to call long distance, you rang the local operator (one short, if I remember correctly), and she would connect you to a long-distance operator who would make the connection. Early switchboard operators physically worked at a large board with numerous holes for phone jacks. To connect you to another party, they physically inserted a cord from the jack for your phone into a jack for the person to whom you wished to speak. For long-distance calls, they inserted the cord into a long-distance jack and an operator at the other end performed the final connection.

As you can see from the sketch (Figure 4), these phones did not fit in your pocket. Switchboard operators were a vital part of the community in the fifties and sixties.

Figure 4. Party Line with Crank Telephone

First, they were locals who knew most people. Second, they were a source of news and weather. You could call the Moncton operator and ask if it was snowing or whatever. They were also emergency contacts. You could call your local operator, tell her your emergency, and she would contact the appropriate authorities. The local operator knew who was away and likely when they would be back. Ultimately, they were a nexus for community information.[3]

As a 2019 article in *Econ Focus* notes, "An operator did more than simply connect a customer to his or her desired number, however. In the early decades of the industry, telephone companies regarded their business less as a utility and more as a personal service. The telephone operator was central to this idea, acting as an early version of an intelligent assistant with voice recognition capabilities. She got to know her fifty to one hundred assigned customers by name and knew their needs. If a party didn't answer, she would try to find him or her around town. If that didn't succeed, she took a message and called the party again later to pass the message along. She made wake-up calls and gave the time, weather, and sports scores. During crimes in progress or medical emergencies, a subscriber needed only to pick up the handset, and the operator would summon the police or doctors." Eventually, automated switching systems replaced the bulk of operators—convenience and cost-saving, trumping personal service.

Because long-distance calls were so expensive, we used them sparingly. My relatives in the United States figured out how to communicate while avoiding long-distance charges. Here's how it worked: My cousin Betty, who would be driving up from the United States, placed a collect call to Betty Irving at our house. We would tell the operator that she wasn't there. Betty would say that she "would call back at noon tomorrow" and hang up.

---
[3] "Goodbye, Operator," *Econ Focus*, 2019, richmondfed.org.

We would know she would arrive at noon tomorrow—all for free.

We had a car and visited relatives and friends around southern New Brunswick. Most of the roads were not paved and were treacherous in winter. The cars in the fifties and sixties were massive brutes with large engines and terrible gas mileage. Dad traded every year and frequently owned Buicks that got about thirteen miles to the gallon. Of course, gas was only $0.27/gallon then. Because the roads were poor and the vehicles were prone to breakdowns, we always carried an emergency kit, including tools, shovels, chains for the tires, some candles, and matches. Dad always had a spare tire, a spare inner tube repair kit, and a set of tools in the car. Flat tires were frequent.

===

Local Life

When I was a small boy, life was divided clearly into "his" and "her" work. My mother and grandmother did the cooking and cleaning. My father worked as a photographer for the Air Force at Number Five Supply Depot in Moncton, and he did all the outdoor work (except for the garden, which was a shared responsibility with my mother). Our lives changed in 1956 when the Depot closed, and my dad was unemployed for a year. During that year, he took a correspondence course in television repair, with some notion of setting up a repair business. It never happened. Instead, he took a job as a maintenance foreman at T.P. Downey and Sons Lumber, where he remained until he retired.

We were closely connected socially to our small community. It'd been known originally as "Irving Settlement": named after my great-great-grandfather George Irving (an early settler). The name was changed in the early 1900s when a cartographer happened to ask a local, who—for some reason—told him the place was named Baltimore. He probably thought there were too many Irvings out and about. In Baltimore (as I knew it), there were seven families: four Irvings (all related, of course), two Steeves, and one Gaudette. The name change caused some community rancour that resonated for fifty years. My simplified map (Figure 5) shows the layout of Baltimore with key elements noted.

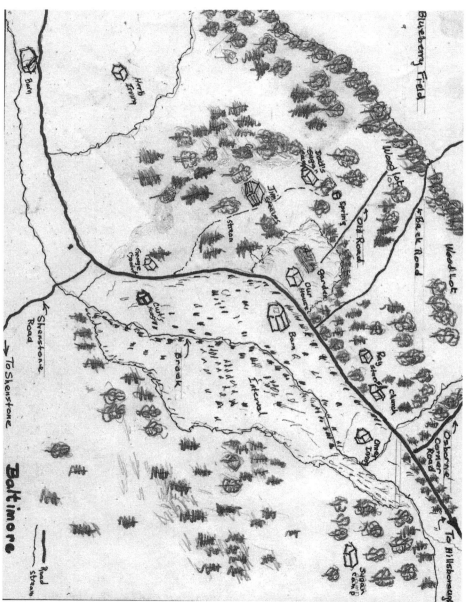

Figure 5. Map of Baltimore

My People[4]

George Irving (the first Irving in Albert County) was born in Dumfries, Scotland (1788), and died in Baltimore (1841). He married Agnes McWhirr in 1811 and sailed to Saint John, New Brunswick, in 1817; eventually settling in Musquash. From there, he ran coastal schooners for several years. George and Agnes had eight children, the youngest of whom was James Irving (my great-grandfather). In 1827, George set out for Baltimore with his twelve-year-old son (William), and built a log cabin. The rest of the family joined them the following year.

Great-grandfather James was the most religious of the family. He was instrumental in founding the Baptist church in Baltimore, where he served as its minister. In 1854, he married Eliza Steeves. Their wedding picture (Figure 6) shows two serious-looking folks.

James and Eliza had thirteen children: seven boys and six girls. Eliza Steeves was related to William Henry Steeves, a father of Confederation. So, we have an indirect connection to history, if not to fame. There are other Irvings in New Brunswick who are famous—K.C. Irving created a business empire that included pulp

Figure 6. Wedding, James Irving and Eliza Steeves

and paper; oil and gas; and shipping. The Irving family is very prominent in New Brunswick as one of the wealthiest families in Canada. There is no connection between us—except for sharing a last name and roots in Dumfries, Scotland.

My grandfather Sanford (Sandy) was the second oldest of Rev. James Irving's brood. Sandy Irving married my grandmother (Margaret "Maggie" Turner) in 1895 (Figure 7) and, shortly thereafter, built the house where I grew up. My dad (Harold) was the youngest of their eight children. During my time, only five of them

---

[4]The information in this section comes from a variety of sources, including *Funday Family* by William H. Irving (The Seeman Printery, Durham, North Carolina, 1972); *The Family Name Price* by Ralph A. Price (House of Falmouth Inc., Portland, Maine, 1973); *The Descendants of Edmond and Jane (Webb) Price* by F. Amos, G. Keith, and M. Perry (1976); and personal family notes.

were still alive. Aunt Cora, Uncle Bob, and Uncle Reg lived in Connecticut (where the whole family had moved during the Depression). My dad, Uncle Curtis (Curt), and my grandparents all eventually returned to Albert County (Figure 8).

Aunt Cora and Uncle Reg were tall, red-headed, with freckles—and personalities to match. Dad (Harold) was tall, lean, and wiry with a laid-back personality and a wry sense of humour—he liked to tease. Uncle Curt and Uncle Bob were shorter, with blocky builds and quiet dispositions.

Figure 7. Sanford (Sandy) and Margaret (Maggie) Irving

My grandmother (Margaret "Maggie" Turner) is a bit of a blur in my mind. I can remember her reading to me when I was small. Her father (Henry Turner) was born in Binnington, England, in 1835. According to my cousin Elma's notes, he crossed the Atlantic twice: going first to Ohio and then to Ontario and Quebec. He walked down to the Miramichi where he stayed with First Nations people for the winter, then he walked to New Brunswick in the spring sometime during the late 1850s.

Figure 8. Sandy, Maggie, Bob, Curt, and Harold Irving

Ultimately, he obtained a grant on Turner Mountain in Albert County (a few miles from Baltimore), or "Irving Settlement" as it was known (see the family tree, Figure 9).

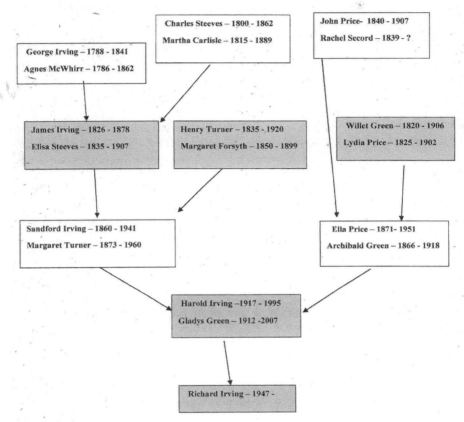

Figure 9: Irving Family Tree

On April 22nd, 1867, he was married to Margaret Forsyth by my grandfather (Rev. James Irving). Subsequently, they had eight children, of whom my grandmother (Maggie) was the third oldest. After her mother's stroke, Maggie took over managing the family and probably raised her siblings. I only knew my great-uncles, William (Bill) and Charles (Charlie).

Figure 10 shows a photo of Margaret Forsyth Turner on the left, probably John Turner in the back, my grandmother Maggie in the front, and Henry on the right.

Grandma Maggie was a petite, severe-looking old lady when I knew her. She kept busy, but there was always time for stories.

Figure 10: Margaret, John, Maggie, and Henry Turner

My mother (Gladys) was short, slim, and had a bustling no-nonsense atmosphere—but she was quiet. I once joked that as an extrovert, it was abusive to be brought up by two introverts. It fell flat.

My grandmother and my mother (you will meet her family soon) got along okay.

They kept busy churning butter, killing chickens, baking, and sewing. In her youth (so Dad told me), Grandma Maggie served as a midwife to most of the women who gave birth in the local area and as a "practical nurse." That is a nurse with no formal medical training but a lot of experience. She once told me how her brother, my Uncle Bill (quite a character, you'll meet him later), somehow managed to sever his toes with an axe. Since they were still connected, she cleaned the wound and put the foot on a clean cedar shingle, wrapping it tightly. They healed properly.

One of Grandma Maggie's stories that I remember well is how she and her two brothers were alone one day (in their log cabin on Turner Mountain) when they saw someone coming through the woods. Now, they had heard stories of Indigenous people stealing children and other horrors. Today, we know that was nonsense, but they were frightening tales in those days. The children all crept up to the loft and hid. The guy walked into the cabin, looked around, and left. Afterward, they decided that perhaps he wasn't so "dangerous" after all.

Three other Irving families were living in Baltimore. The first two families were headed by brothers Omer—his wife Beatrice (Bea), and their daughter Garda—and Herbert (Herb), with his wife Dawn, and their five children.

Omer and Herb were the sons of Scott Irving and descendants of George N. Irving (a brother of great-grandfather, James Irving). Omer was my dad's cousin, and lived with his family about a mile southeast of us in George N.'s old homestead. Omer and Herb were both relatively short. Omer was a rotund guy with an energetic personality.

He provoked easily, which meant Dad and Herb delighted in winding him up. Herb was small and wiry with a talent for exaggeration.

Bea and my mother were friends, as were Garda and I. Bea was my teacher for seven of my eight grades (Figure 11).

Figure 11. Gladys, Richard, Maggie, Garda, Bea, and Omer Irving

The third family consisted of Uncle Curt and his wife Elvira, along with their son Jimmy. Jimmy was much older than me, so I did not know him well; unfortunately, I have little contact with his family.

In addition to the three Irving families, rounding out the settlement were George Gaudet with his wife (Marion); Ray Steeves with Iola (and their two children); and Ray's brother (Jim Steeves), who lived near us in a log cabin.

That was my world as a small child.

Since we lived in Grandfather Sandy's "Old Homestead," everyone came back to our place for hunting season, as well as Thanksgiving, Christmas, and summer trips. Combined with my mother's four siblings, there was considerable activity at my home when I was small. After my grandmother died in 1955, the visits became less frequent but never stopped entirely.

In a small, tight-knit community like Baltimore, people knew you by your family. Decades later, as a grown man with a son (Alex), people in Hillsborough still introduced me to strangers as "Harold's boy." I recently had a "Circle of Life" moment when I was referred to as "Alex's Dad" in a meeting.

Our big trips were usually to my mother's old homestead on the Saint John River located five kilometres south of Evendale, New Brunswick (Figure 12). Given the state of the back roads in the fifties and sixties, this 150 km (96 miles) trip took about three or four hours. Now, of course, it takes about two hours.

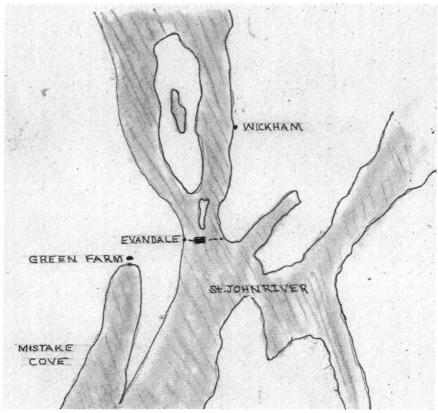

Figure 12. Saint John River at Evandale

The farm was at the head of Mistake Cove about five kilometres south of Evandale on the Saint John River—Edmond Price established it in 1779. He had moved to New Brunswick from Wales in 1767 (Figure 13). Ella Gertrude Price (my maternal grandmother) was born May 29, 1871, on the farm near Mistake Cove, New Brunswick. She married her third cousin (Archibald Menzes Green) on June 1, 1904. He died of stomach cancer in 1918, leaving Ella with five children ranging in ages from four to fourteen years old plus a farm to run.

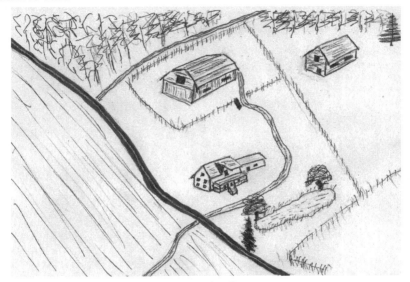

Figure 13. The Green Farm at Mistake Cove

My mother Gladys was the second youngest; her sister Georgie was the youngest.

Mom and Georgie were both short and slim with dark hair. Aunt Georgie eventually became one of the first female computer programmers at the National Research Council in Ottawa.

Aunt Muriel and Aunt Elsie were the oldest and second oldest, respectively. Both were tall, with Aunt Muriel being slender and Aunt Elsie being more robust. Uncle Ken was the middle child and took over running the farm. Possibly because of the war, Aunt Muriel, Uncle Ken, and Aunt Georgie never married. Aunt Muriel became a schoolteacher, as did my mother. Aunt Muriel, a good-hearted soul, was the epitome of the spinster schoolteacher. She was tall, thin, and was easily agitated—something at which her four nephews excelled.

Mom and Aunt Elsie (who raised three boys and one girl) were much calmer and more relaxed, perhaps because they were married and had families. Aunt Georgie (being a single professional woman when this wasn't common) was a tough lady. She was kind and loving to her family, but she had strong opinions and was more than willing to share them with you.

Uncle Ken was the perfect image of an old farmer. His weather-beaten, permanently tanned face reflected the hard outdoor life he led. Ken had a crooked smile as a result of being kicked by a cow. He and Aunt Muriel lived on the old homestead, and she supported the farm through her teaching. The photo shows him giving my cousins Amanda and Sylvia a ride on his plough horse (Figure 14).

Figure 14. Uncle Ken with Sylvia and Amanda Sauerman

I remember listening to the four sisters working in the kitchen when we had a big dinner at the farm. To say it was loud would be an understatement.

Usually, Aunt Muriel and Aunt Georgie would be arguing

vociferously—and mother and Aunt Elsie would be trying to calm things down (Figure 15).

Once I remember my mother telling her: "Muriel, just because you didn't get your way does *not* mean the world is ending."

Figure 15. The Green Sisters: Georgie, Gladys, Elsie, and Muriel

At one family gathering in the early seventies, all four nephews showed up with full beards. Aunt Muriel loudly expressed her displeasure. When we left and kissed her goodbye, each nephew brushed their beard against her cheek.

Chapter 2

The Old Homestead

Our homestead in Baltimore consisted of about four hundred acres with a farmhouse, barn, two fields, and an extensive wood lot containing hardwoods and softwoods. Our house sat on a sidehill with a cleared area running up the slope to the edge of our forest. The forest ran uphill until it touched the blueberry plains at the top of the hill (see Figure 5).

Below the house, the land sloped down to the main road. The barn was across the road, behind it was a brook (an arm of Turtle Creek) that ran the valley's length. Behind the stream was a cleared stretch of land (or interval) that ran out to the hill beyond where the forest began.

To this day, the smell of spruce trees, mixed with the aroma of grass, dust, and wood smoke, immediately takes me back to my home in Baltimore.

===

The Farmhouse

The old farmhouse that my grandfather built was a wooden-framed, two-story house with wood clapboards and cedar shingles (Figure 16). Since they had no ready access to tar paper, large sheets of birch bark covered the framing boards under the clapboards. Using birch bark in this way was a traditional method that provided good wind-proofing and cheap insulation. However, it wasn't fireproof, a fact we came to regret much later.

Figure 16. The Original Irving Homestead

The house had a large front porch and a summer kitchen. The first floor encompassed a large kitchen and pantry, a dining room, and a parlour. Most of the family life took place in the kitchen. Upstairs were four bedrooms. The basement (largely unfinished) was used for storing preserves, vegetables, and sometimes meat. For example, we used one bin to store potatoes, which we covered in sand. That kept them edible for most of the winter, although we did look forward to the first new potatoes.

Summer kitchens were a regular feature of farmhouses in the early 1900s. The summer kitchen (which was a rudimentary addition) contained a worktable, a stove, and a pantry. We used it for cooking during hot weather to avoid heating the rest of the house. In the winter, it provided cold storage.

Another way to keep the house cool on hot days was to pull the drapes on the sunward side and open windows on the shady side. As the sun moved during the day, my mother would open and close the windows and drapes to match. The interior of the house was shaded and relatively cool. Having a veranda and overhanging eaves also helped. Part of a good house design was situating your home to get shade in summer and sun in winter. Because there was no central heating or air conditioning, we were very attuned to the weather and the seasons.

We also had a water pump in a small room beside the back door, a large woodshed, and an outhouse behind the main building. No reason to linger there in winter for sure. Not much reason to loiter in summer either, as it was wonderfully aromatic and housed some of the largest spiders I have ever seen.

The woodshed, which connected the summer kitchen and the outhouse, had to be large since all our heating used wood. Typically, we would have collected ten to twelve cords of wood before the first snowfall in late October, cut and neatly stacked in the woodshed for proper drying and easy retrieval.

Fire safety was always an issue. One cord of wood is four-feet wide, four-feet high, and eight-feet long. Imagine twelve cords of dry wood (with all the inevitable bark, sawdust, and wood chips) piled beside your house. Everyone smoked, and a single discarded cigarette butt could set it all alight. We were all exceedingly careful about sparks in the woodshed. As you might guess, house fires were common—I grew up in the second house on the property, the first having burned down much earlier…and it was *not* the last one to do so.

We had no indoor plumbing, electricity, or central heating until around 1955. In our kitchen sat a large icebox where we could keep milk (and anything else that needed cooling). An "iceman" came around now and then, who'd sell us a large block of ice that could last for a week or two. There was a large wood stove in the kitchen for cooking and a small stove in the living room for heating—that was it!

As the warmest room (and the largest), the kitchen was the social centre of the house.

It ran the length of the house, featuring a pantry at the east end, with a stove, an old couch, and a table with some chairs at the west end. In the evenings, the family (and visitors) tended to congregate there to work, talk, and hang out until it was time to "have a lunch" and go to bed. From "Figure 17," you can see the wood box to the left of the stove. The stove itself had a fire door on the left side (where you piled in wood), an oven, a water tank to the right (for warm water), and a warming oven above the stove (to keep plates and food warm). The stovepipe ran up through the stove to an outlet that connected it to the chimney.

Figure 17. The Old Kitchen

We used different terms for meals than are common now. Our noon meal was "dinner," and the evening meal was "supper." About 3 p.m., we had "a cup of tea"—(fancy people had 'tea,' I guess). By about 9 p.m., we had a "lunch" (or what most of us would call a snack before bed—usually just a cup of tea and a biscuit or square).

The bedrooms were only heated with the residual heat from the stoves below, in the kitchen or parlour. I remember being chilly in winter (then very warm in summer) when I was about four or five. My bedroom received only a little heat from downstairs, but we had two other tricks to keep warm!

The first trick was a hot water bottle: You filled it with water as hot as you could stand, then put it under the covers about a half-hour before you got into bed. The second was heavy woollen blankets with flannel sheets. In winter, you would run up the stairs, change into flannel pyjamas, and jump quickly into bed—pulling the covers over your head.

In the morning, you reversed the process: The trick was to put your socks on in bed. On the coldest mornings, you tried to get dressed entirely in bed as well. Getting dressed entailed stripping off your flannel pyjamas and quickly pulling on your long johns—which are like full-body underwear with a trap door in the rear, so you could answer "Nature's Call" without getting all undressed in the cold. Long johns were followed quickly by home-made clothing: wool socks, wool pants, and a flannel shirt.

Under each bed was a chamber pot. If you had to go in the middle of the night, that is what you used—God help you if you tipped it over. Naturally, they were emptied daily. Luckily, we managed to get indoor plumbing before I was old enough to have that job!

Oil lamps provided our only source of light. We had two types at home: simple oil lamps and "Aladdin" lamps. Simple oil lamps featured just a glass frame to hold oil, with a wick and a glass chimney. They gave some light but tended to be smoky. One major trick with regular oil lamps was to trim the wicks so that they didn't smoke. A lamp with a poorly trimmed wick could smoke up the house—to the point where there would be a black spot on the ceiling.

Aladdin lamps had a unique filament that allowed them to burn quite brightly with little smoke. It was relatively easy to read by an Aladdin lamp because it was about as bright as a sixty-watt bulb. I remember how the lamps gave everything a golden glow, creating mysterious shadows in the room's corners. But they also presented the constant danger of someone knocking over a lamp, thus, starting a fire. While we never had that problem, many houses burned down because of this type of accident, and very few folks had fire insurance.

Figure 18. An Aladdin Lamp

===

The Barn

One way you can tell a good farmer is to look at the barn and the house. If the barn is in better shape than the house, he is a good farmer. If both are in good condition, he is a wealthy farmer. Back in the fifties, in Albert County, there were many of the former but few of the latter.

Grandpa Sandy built our barn: He used large hand-cut timbers for the frame and connected them with mortise and tenon joints joined with wooden pegs. That is an ancient method in which the builder joins two pieces of wood by cutting a hole or groove into one (the "mortise"), and a projection on the other (the "tenon") as shown in Figure 19). When Dad and I tore down the barn to build a garage years later, the frame of the old barn was so solid that he had to use a chainsaw to take it apart. Since then, I have learned that the mortise-and-tenon method Grandpa used

Figure 19. A Mortise and Tenon Joint with Wooden Peg

is *exceptionally* robust. Because no iron is used, there is no rust and little rotting of the wood. Also, these structures can flex a bit, making them resistant to earthquakes and high winds.

Our barn was in reasonable repair in the early fifties (Figure 20). It featured three or four stalls for cattle, though we only used one. There were two haylofts (a high one and a lower one), standing remnants of the days when we had more than one cow. Behind the barn was the inevitable manure pile—free fertilizer!

Figure 20: Our Old Barn

Most barns (that I knew of) had a small herd of barn cats to keep the mice under control, and ours was no exception. These were semi-feral cats—*not* house pets. Once, I tried to tame a barn cat as a house pet…it did not go well. The damned thing regularly crapped on my bed. One day, I was petting it and put my face close to the cat. It hit me with its paw so hard, it left a bruise. Fortunately, it kept its claws retracted, or there would have been some serious damage. That experiment ended abruptly, and the cat was retired back to the barn and never invited into the house again.

The other occupants of the barn in spring and summer were barn swallows. They were most welcome, as they were voracious eaters of mosquitoes and other insects. Barn swallows are very protective of their nests and will swoop down on anyone who comes near them. Naturally, they did not make friends with the cats.

Barn cats are aggressive predators who will attempt to eat whatever they can catch. The swallows made their nests high in the eaves of the barn, safely away from any predators.

However, the cats were always watchful. I used to watch the cats jump and try to catch the swallows as they swooped up and down. The swallows seemed to enjoy teasing the cats by continually flying just out of reach. The cats would jump and repeatedly miss until, in disgust, they would sit and stare balefully at the swallows.

In the late 1950s, we noticed that there were fewer and fewer swallows. Eventually, we came to know this was because of DDT spraying to kill spruce budworms (an insect considered to be a serious threat to forests in Eastern Canada). In the early 1960s, I read Rachel Carson's *Silent Spring* regarding the effects of pesticides on wildlife. DDT caused the swallows to lay thin-shelled eggs, which were easily broken.[5]

The barn also had a small workshop with an assortment of tools, plus a big blacksmith's vice attached to one corner of the workbench. The barn had the warm, fusty smell of cows, the dusty smell of hay, and the tangy smell of old manure.

Since only two cows occupied the barn, there was lots of room on the main floor for a workshop and as parking for our car. This was useful as we had a long, uphill laneway that got very icy in the winter. Many Saturday afternoons, I was deputised to "help" my father as he worked on the car. To this day, I hate working on a car (or other similar equipment).

The Church

The centre of most social life was the Baptist church (Figure 21). It was a one-story building with a steeply pitched roof, built by my great-grandfather James (who you may remember was a Baptist minister in addition to being a farmer). The church held at most twenty to thirty people. On Wednesday nights, they held prayer meetings and on Sunday mornings, a sermon.

Wednesday night prayer meetings were a *particular* form of torture for a small active boy. For some reason, my mother insisted I go with her until I was

Figure 21. Baptist Church Built by Rev. James Irving

---
[5]Rachel Carson, *Silent Spring* (Penguin Classics, 2000).

old enough to plead homework (or some other excuse). It was torturous because all they did at a prayer meeting was pray—duh! Each matron tried to outdo the other in the length and inclusiveness of her prayers. Fortunately, there were only five or six of them, plus the minister.

But *God*, how they could pray.

Once they had covered family and friends, prayers expanded globally to include the royal family (of course), the prime minister (if he were Conservative), missionaries, and the heathens they saved. Thank God they didn't know all the heathens by name. As you can imagine, a kid did not take well to sitting quietly and listening to the "old ladies" blather on. I took to faking earaches and tummy-aches to avoid the agony. And this worked—sometimes.

Sunday sermons varied widely in length and interest depending on the minister. In my time, we shared a minister with Dawson settlement and a couple of other small communities.

The sermons emphasised the wages of sin (bad!), the rewards of Heaven (good!), and the need to repent (always!). Occasionally, we would get a minister who was a bit better educated than the norm, and they would produce a sermon that was more like a history lesson. I rather enjoyed those—but I was in the minority. Most of the congregation wanted hellfire and brimstone in their sermons…and long, creative prayers.

The one thing that I did enjoy at a Baptist service was the singing. There was a lot of it, and most people could sing. It was also a popular form of evening entertainment. Almost every farmhouse had musical instruments, and someone who knew how to play them. In our house, we had a small organ, a guitar, and a violin. My dad (along with all his brothers and sisters) could sing and play. Dad learned to play by ear; he could do a passable job on the organ, violin, and guitar. But he was by no means unique. I remember visiting neighbours to spend most of the evening singing old songs, or listening to "the Old Folks" tell stories of days past. Of course, those "old folks" were probably twenty years younger than I am now.

One reason Baptists are so-named is that they fully immerse people in water. My church used complete immersion in a river—during summer, thankfully. At twelve years old, I had reached the "Age of Reason" (at least, for Baptists). At that time (1959), I was expected to declare my belief in Jesus and my commitment to the Church. Growing up where I did (coupled with social pressure from the community), there was no other option…so I went along with it—even though I had decided most of what I heard in church was bollocks!

Let's be clear, my problem was (and remains with) theology. The church, as a social institution, served (and serves) an essential role in creating a cohesive community. First, it provided a reason to stop working one day each week, get together with your neighbours, and to think about something other than yourself. Second, it created a mechanism whereby the community could come together to celebrate events, mourn losses, and work on joint projects. Generally, it was a social and political hub for the community and a force for good. When folks were much more isolated than now (with far less access to information), it provided a centre around which communities were created and sustained. In some places, it still plays that role.

On the Sunday of the big event, a few other people and I were baptised in a stream about five miles from our church. Eventually, I was led to the water wearing jeans and a t-shirt; the minister lay me on my back and fully immersed me in the water. My first thought was, *I hope he lets me up*. Fortunately, I had the presence of mind to keep my heathen thoughts to myself as I survived to become a full-fledged member of the church. After I was baptised, my mother wrapped me in a big towel and helped me change my clothes. And then the service continued, though I remember nothing of it.

While I have lived away from the community since 1967, my cousin recently informed me that (through attrition), I had technically become a deacon in the Baltimore Baptist Church. Oh, the irony!

OK…so, let's deal with this religious issue. I am not arrogant enough to be an atheist, nor am I compliant enough to be a true believer. If there is an organising force to the universe, I expect it is far beyond our comprehension (and doubt that it cares what we wear on our heads or eat). But it *is* conceivable that its spiritual emanations are widely broadcasted—and that some humans are capable of receiving them. Much like some people can see colours that others do not or hear sounds that those of us with tin ears don't recognize.

This concept of emanation was described to me over lunch with Karen Armstrong, an author and a well-known professor of theology.[6] She explained emanation as the ability of some people to sense the spiritual emanations of the guiding spirit of the universe. Being imperfectly able to comprehend them, they filter these emanations through their gender, social norms, language and customs, and develop religious pronouncements which form the basis of our major religious traditions. It makes sense to me, though I am as spiritually deaf as I am tone deaf. When I asked her, "Why have I not heard about this before; why is it not discussed widely?"

Her response was to the point: "No one ever went to war because of emanations!"

If you accept the premise, then all religions have some smidgeon of ultimate truth at their core and encompass a vast body of social norms, nonsense, and political control disguised as faith. In the end, I believe we need to search for the common good in all religions—and eschew the political and fundamentalist dogma in which it is embedded.

Thus, endeth the lesson: Let's move on to more fun stuff!

===

Socialising

When my father was young, it was common in winter for the community to gather on the top floor of the Baltimore schoolhouse and put on "entertainments." Some folks would sing and play, others would recite poetry. At the same time, those of a more dramatic bent would perform one-act plays and skits. Everyone was expected to perform something. This is a level of conviviality that we have mostly lost today. Sadly, in my time, the old schoolhouse had fallen into disuse. Television became common, and the custom withered away.

A common social event was "dropping in for an evening cup of tea." A neighbour would show up with their family during the early evening, say around 7:30 p.m. Just drop by. We would hang out and talk—usually about weather, crops, and politics. Around 8:30 p.m.,

---

[6]Karen Armstrong, *A History of God* (Alfred A Knopf, 1993). See also, https://en.wikipedia.org/wiki/Karen_Armstrong.

my mother would ask: "Would you like a cup of tea?"

To which the standard reply was: "Oh no! We have got to get going."

After three or four of these, back and forth, they (of course) would stay—and mother would set out some tea with the inevitable "squares."

Now, to you, a square is a small, tasty, rectangular sweet. But for us at that time, squares were also culinary statements. Each lady competed with the others to develop the most interesting and delectable squares imaginable. Some were truly wonderful, others not so much.

If one of the local matrons found (or created) a fabulous square recipe, this was a major coup that engendered vigorous discussion and much credit. That house would get regular visits on Saturday nights, for several weeks, until the crowd moved elsewhere. If the result was a flop, no one said anything. But the silence was deafening—and the poor woman would slink off, resolving to win the next battle. If you go to Hillsborough today and are lucky enough to be invited for dinner (or "tea"), there will still be squares!

The kids and menfolk all *quietly* encouraged this competitive spirit.

Another area of great competition for the ladies was producing dishes for church socials. Each lady had a couple of standard recipes that she regularly provided. Poor cooks were regarded with pity and charitably tolerated. Good cooks were celebrated! Church socials were much more than fundraisers for the church. The social was where the locals discussed politics, resolved (and sometimes created) disputes, and shared the latest gossip.

A final area of social competition was "having the minister for dinner." I felt sorry for the poor souls. Not only did they have to endure many nights out and a wide range of cooking; but they also had to be positive, no matter what, and endure stilted conversations while the families put on "company manners." Naturally, these evenings always involved some spiritual counselling and prayers. Since social services were virtually nonexistent, the minister was often the only one who could intervene in family or psychological problems.

Kids, especially, got an earful on how to behave. God help any child who misspoke in front of the parson—trust me, *I know*. Having a child who asks authority figures logical but awkward questions such as "How do you know God exists?" is a trial for parents. I have experienced this truth from both sides.

====

Religious Divide

Albert County (where we lived) was primarily white, Protestant, and English-speaking. Westmoreland County, just across the Petitcodiac River, was primarily French and Catholic. Being a homogeneous mix of religion, language, and ethnic background, we didn't trust "those other folks" across the river who spoke a different language and had a different faith. My mother (coming as she did from Loyalists and Orangemen) was very distrustful of French Catholics. Not actually knowing any Catholics or Frenchmen didn't help.

In the 1950s, in Moncton, there was one Chinese restaurant and one Jewish family. I never saw a Black person until I was about ten years old…though, I did meet some Indigenous folks who came to the area to pick blueberries at the commercial field up over the hill. The Chief's sons took two puppies from the same litter as my dog. When they came by, we would play with the dogs. Other than that interaction, I learned nothing about Indigenous peoples at school—our history classes barely mentioned them. They also failed to mention that William Henry Steeves, a father of Confederation and an ancestor, was from Hillsborough. We did learn *a lot* about British history, though.

While things eventually changed for me, it was many years before things changed politically in New Brunswick. Some of the misunderstandings and mistrust still lingers. In the fifties, religion and politics were intertwined, particularly in Albert County. In those days, we Protestants in Albert County mostly voted Conservative…while the French Canadians across the river in Westmoreland County mostly voted Liberal. Of course, there was some overlap on both sides. Political affiliation became important when the government changed and patronage jobs were handed out.

In rural Albert County, the patronage jobs were primarily road work. If the Liberals were in power, Liberals tended to get hired; the reverse was true if Conservatives took over. This situation wasn't unique to that time or place and *is* still practised today—albeit a bit more subtly. In those days, however, it was blatant and accepted:

Our team won; I got a job!

Things Change

Most of the changes that affected rural Albert County were a consequence of developments that swept Canada as a whole, though they were slower in the Maritimes. Improved rail service allowed the relatively quick transport of goods across the country. Improved roads allowed for more reliable transportation by truck and car. It also encouraged people to live farther from work and to travel for leisure much more often than in the past.

The rural electrification program brought energy into the homes of most of New Brunswick by the close of the 1950s. Television penetrated our homes by the end of the fifties, bringing the world into our living rooms and expanded how we saw our world.

But as the fifties ended and our world continued to expand, our local economic opportunities dwindled. Number Five Supply Depot was closed as the Air Force reduced its presence in Moncton, putting my father out of work. The CNR shops where my Uncle Curt worked for many years moved elsewhere. By the mid-1960s, it was clear that unless you wanted to cut logs, fish, or farm, you had to go elsewhere.

As the fifties bled into the sixties and then into the seventies, life began to change even more rapidly. The most noticeable effect of improved transportation was the increasing availability of fruits and vegetables. When my parents were small, an orange was a rare treat. By the end of the fifties, TV dinners were readily available, as were frozen fruits and vegetables. The roads were mostly still dirt, but they were in better condition. Sometimes, the electricity went out, but less frequently than before. TVs were common, and people began to travel a bit more.

Furthermore, as Canada began to encourage immigration, more people came to New Brunswick, bringing new languages, religions, and customs to what had been an insular province.

So *that* is the time and place in which I grew up. It was insular and conservative but very connected and supportive. If you heard a neighbour was in financial trouble, you might drop off some "extra" potatoes, apples, or beef. If someone needed help with the farm, there were usually volunteers. We looked after each other because the pioneer habits of self-sufficiency and taking care of each other were still strong. Religion was central, the family was everything, and community was important. Things were stable, the future looked positive—but changes were coming.

Part 2

My Albert County Years in Four Seasons

Living when and where I did, life flowed more around the seasons than around the years. Our lives (like the land) changed with the seasons; each season provided its food, fun, and work. In spring, we planted; in summer, we tended; in fall, we harvested; and in winter, we recuperated, repaired, and mended for the coming spring.

As the first spring shoots reached through melting snow to grasp the warmth of the early sun, we'd emerge from our own winter's sleep to the promise of warmer days and fresh beginnings. Away went the snow shovels, off came the heavy coats and boots, and a new cycle began in Albert County.

Chapter 3

Spring Renewal

Spring started slowly in Baltimore. Though winter formally ended around March 19th or 20th, winter lingered at our place nestled in the valley below the hills.

The transition to spring happened slowly and gradually from mid-March to about mid-May. I remember seeing snow at the edges of the woods until May, though it was gone from the fields. When spring finally arrived, it was very welcome.

We would usually see the snow begin to diminish slightly by late March. We'd have a few days when the temperature would climb above freezing, but many more when it did not. Even if it warmed up during the day, the nights would be cold. It was about this time that people started thinking about making maple sugar.

You could almost feel warmth in the air when the sun was out. The slight thawing during the day and freezing at night produced heavy crusts. It was fun to run around on top of snow you'd been sinking into before. Of course, it was perfect for sledding! I would take my sled or toboggan to the top of our hill and fly down again and again. After school, I would do this until dark (or suppertime, whichever came first). Occasionally, I did it by moonlight—a magical and spooky experience.

The tops of the maples provided another good harbinger of spring. If you looked carefully, you could perceive a slight haze—not actual buds, but the promise of buds. As March became April, the warmer days became more frequent, and the buds grew larger.

Sugar Season

The first *big* spring event was the maple sugar season, which ran roughly from mid-March to mid-April (depending on the weather). To get the sap flowing well, you needed days when the temperature rose above freezing and nights when it dropped well below freezing. Some years, Mother Nature cooperated better than others.

Sugar season was one of the first opportunities for farmers to earn some hard cash—and they took advantage of it. I remember Omer Irving telling us how he drove into the United States to sell maple syrup in Boston at the end of the season. You only needed your driver's licence or birth certificate to cross the border back then. This looseness lasted until 9/11. I remember flying into New York from Toronto in the mid-eighties with only my credit card for identification. Good luck trying that today.

The local market absorbed most of the syrup and sugar production. Almost everyone who had a few maple trees collected sap and made syrup. We were all involved, be it a gallon or two for home use, or a full-scale commercial production.

New Brunswick has a long history of sugar production and is the world's third-largest producer of maple sugar and syrup. The colonists originally learned how to make this sweet treat from the Indigenous inhabitants of New Brunswick. We took to the process with gusto.[7]

===

Omer's Sugar Camp

The first memories I have are visiting (and later working at) the sugar camp owned by Omer Irving. Omer's camp was about half a kilometre back in the woods. Like most sugar camps, it was at the bottom of a hill near a stream. His daughter Garda recently informed me that one year there were 3,500 taps. Since one large tree might have three or four taps inserted, this would be around 1,000 trees.

---

[7] According to an article in the *Dalhousie Review*, there is evidence of sugar production along the Saint John River dating from prehistoric times. The writer goes on to state, "In one of the bulletins of the New Brunswick Historical Society, mention is found that Jean Baptiste Cyr, Acadian colonist of 1770 in what is now York County, N. B., was an early commercial sugar producer."

The trees were all tapped by hand, using a brace-and-bit drill and a hammer. You bored a small hole into the tree with the hand drill, then gently inserted a spile (which was a tapered, hollow metal plug with a hook to which you could attach a pail). A can with a lid was hung on the spile, and then on you went to the next one. Assuming five minutes for each one, 3,500 taps would take about 17,500 minutes (or 291 work hours). Three men, working eight hours per day, would take twelve days to tap all the trees.

And this was just the beginning of the work.

We usually arrived at the camp on a sled pulled by two horses. The sled would carry three or four people with all the supplies we needed that day. Now, when they see a picture of people sitting on a sled pulled by horses, most folks think: *Wow, romantic!*

The *reality* was quite different. The horses were in the barn all winter. Pulling the sled was hard work and seemed to upset their digestive systems. Remember, we were on a low-slung sled right behind the horses. We choked our way to the sugar camp in a cloud of horse farts.

Once at the camp, Omer and my dad would unload the sled and fire up the evaporator. It was a long, narrow, wood-fueled firebox, covered by three evaporator trays that were laid end to end. We poured raw sap into the first tray, and as it evaporated, it would be syphoned to the next tray—and so on. The last tray contained syrup. Since it took roughly one cord of wood to produce ten gallons of syrup, Omer went through ten to twelve cords of wood most years.

One of the first things we did in the morning was head out to collect the sap. At Omer's sugar camp, we did this by hand. In April, it would have been below freezing at night and would usually be above freezing during the day. In the early morning, there was a hard crust to walk on.

Figure 22: Collecting Sap

First thing, we headed out, each carrying two, five-gallon pails.

We walked to the top of the hill and began to fill our buckets from the sap pails hanging from the furthest trees. Usually, the first trip or two went well. We headed back down to the sugar camp when the buckets were full and dumped the sap into a large, galvanised-steel collection tank. This tank fed the raw sap to the evaporator.

Since snowshoes were a bit awkward, we tried to avoid them if possible. However: by around 11:00 a.m., things were warming up. Inevitably, some poor fellow would be heading back with two heavy pails filled with sap when the crust gave way and down he'd plunge up to his waist. The pails would land on the crust and tip over, filling his rubber boots with sap. He spent the rest of the day in sticky socks. At that point, we all switched to snowshoes, and the collection proceeded until we gathered all the sap—or it stopped running, usually around 4:00 p.m.

Back at the camp, Omer and the guys stoked the evaporator and checked the temperature of the liquid in the syrup pan. There was always some debate about how much syrup versus sugar to make. This debate was not trivial. It takes around fifty gallons of sap to make a gallon of syrup and about five gallons of syrup to make one pound of sugar. Naturally, you made both, but the proportion of one versus the other depended on likely demand and the price you would get for each.

One perk of working in the sugar camp was having a ladle of sap or syrup whenever you wanted. After two days of indulgence, we rarely used that opportunity.

Easter often came along during the sugar season. When I was small, this was a mainly religious event. The chicks, chocolate bunnies, and Easter eggs came later. Our little church would plan an Easter service, and the church ladies would decorate the church with a mix of natural and paper flowers. Since this was a Baptist church, there was also lots of singing. The sermons were all about resurrection and renewal—a chance to start over. They were long, and sometimes, bordered on the incoherently emotional. Pastors worked themselves into a froth about repentance, salvation, and faith. Perhaps this increased the take from collections. Even as a young boy, I mostly rejected the overtly emotional exhortations: Give me some facts and analysis instead. There was no talk of emanation—it was all received wisdom.

Naturally, there would be a large Easter dinner for friends and family. Ham usually featured prominently, As well as baked goods—lots of baked goods. Hot cross buns were a favourite! I always looked for the ones with the most frosting. The tantalising smell of warm pastry, sugar, and cinnamon fresh from the oven still takes me back to my mother's kitchen. Oddly, there was little or no lamb. My father explained that sheep and goats were common at one time, but because of a Commonwealth agreement whereby Australia and New Zealand would supply lamb and mutton, and Canada would supply pork and beef, the prevalence of these animals declined on our farms. I haven't been able to verify this independently, but it seems plausible.

For me, the best part of Easter was time off school. We usually got about a week off around Easter; but some folks took more time if they had to help in the sugar woods (or generally around the farm).

===

Making Syrup "Old Style"

One Easter vacation (when I was about sixteen), I convinced my friend Paul to join me in making maple syrup the old-fashioned way: boiling sap in a large cast-iron pot over a fire until it became syrup. I had obtained a cast-iron kettle that would hold about fifteen gallons. We hauled it on a sled up a back road to the base of our sugar woods. Our spot was on a flat patch of ground near a brook. The next step was to wander around and tap about a hundred trees, which took about a day or so. We set up a tripod consisting of three stout poles lashed together and hung the kettle from a chain suspended from the tripod's top. Underneath the pot, we would eventually build a fire (Figure 23).

The next day we returned and got to work. And work it was.

First, we had to cut wood for the fire. Given that we only had a bucksaw and an axe, it was a tedious chore that kept us

Figure 23: Making Maple Syrup Old Style

continually busy. We collected sap which we poured into a galvanised tank. Once the kettle was about half full, we started the fire and waited for it to boil. We boiled and boiled and boiled and boiled. Boiling a kettle of sap over an open fire is very inefficient as most of the heat escapes. It *is* fun to watch, though!

After two weeks of laborious work, we had about five gallons of syrup (about twenty-two litres—enough to fill a standard household pail). This was the output after boiling sap seven days a week, eight hours per day. When we were not gathering sap or boiling it, we cut wood and fed the fire. Keeping a fire going every day was a full-time job. There was usually a bit of a breeze, and when we did sit down, it seemed that the smoke was always in your face no matter where you sat.

Even though we were about a kilometre back in the woods, we often had visitors.

One by one, the old-timers would drop by to see what we were doing. It took them back to when they were kids, when they watched their fathers make syrup the way we were doing it. The old guys would sit around and tend the fire; while Paul and I cut wood and collected sap. When we had some downtime, they would tell us stories of what it was like when they were our age.

I only made syrup that way one time; it was too much work. However, I think Paul and I inspired my dad to build a sugar camp of his own.

===

Dad's Sugar Camp

In the seventies, Dad decided to build a sugar camp near where Paul and I had placed our pot. He graded a road down to the site and constructed a solid sugar camp. Dad was *not* about to slog around with pails of sap. He got some food-grade plastic hose and created a system where liquid flowed directly into a storage tank from the trees. The sap then poured into the evaporator, and away he went (Figure 24).

I believe that he tapped at least three hundred or four hundred trees…possibly more. It was a lot of work tapping the trees and arranging the hoses to transport the sap. On many occasions, I remember him cursing because a deer (or a moose) had run through the woods and torn down the tubing he had just put up. Despite these setbacks, the whole process worked well.

Figure 24: Dad's Sugar Camp

Twelve years after his death, I visited my cousins in Lorneville. Lo and behold, they brought out some syrup my dad had made many years before. Since it wasn't a commercial operation, Dad boiled the syrup a bit longer than average, thus producing a dark, heavy, and very sweet product. It'd been stored in a refrigerator and was still delicious.

Picking Fiddleheads

As I said, spring in Baltimore came gradually, but come it did, and things began to turn green. One event in late April (or early May) was the arrival of fiddleheads. Fiddleheads are the rolled-up tops of the Ostrich fern found throughout New Brunswick. These ferns begin to emerge in swampy and damp areas and are considered to be a delicacy by many people. Because my mother loved them, I had to help her pick them. We would start on a sunny afternoon, heading for the nearest creek. Mother would pick a shaded marshy area with lots of ground cover.

We would root around under the leaves and find the emerging fiddleheads. Mom's capacity to eat fiddleheads was enormous!

No matter how much I fussed and complained, we stayed until we had a large bag full. Usually, a haul would be about five kilos. Unfortunately, that was also the time of year when black flies started to emerge. They just added to the fun.

When our bags were complete, we hurried home, and mother boiled or steamed a batch and served them for dinner with a bit of salt and vinegar. I couldn't stand them! Though they are considered a gourmet treat, I still don't like them. Today, high-end food shops will sell a small bottle of fiddleheads in vinegar for $10 or more—but not to me!

Figure 25: Picking Fiddleheads

===

May 18th was Arbour Day throughout New Brunswick. This was the day when we (in theory) planted trees. The holiday began in Canada and United States in the mid-1800s, when citizens became concerned about deforestation and were determined to increase the tree cover. In 1884, New Brunswick established Arbour Day to plant trees, a practice that continues to this day.

We didn't see much point in planting trees at our one-room schools since they were surrounded by forest. Instead, we used it as an opportunity to clean up the schoolyard. We raked up old leaves and debris, removed rocks, and generally spruced things up. It was a great time to be outdoors and not in the classroom.

We tidied up our fields around that time as well. By mid-May, most areas were clear of snow and beginning to dry out. Once the grass was dry, we burned it off. The resulting ash fertilized the field.

The trick was to burn the grass before the snow was out of the woods. No one wanted to start a forest fire. You also had to watch the wind direction; more than one house burned when the wind changed.

===

Mid-May was when farmers started to till the soil once it was dry enough. This tilling prepared the ground for planting later.

Victoria Day—Canada's oldest (official) non-religious holiday—was the typical earliest date for planting. It occurs on the last Monday that comes before May 25th; no sensible person planted anything before then. The idea was that you wouldn't risk a significant frost after that date, though I remember Mom and Dad rushing out with sacks (and even blankets) to cover the tomatoes and other delicate plants even after that date.

While cities and towns had fireworks displays for Victoria Day, we made do with a few firecrackers and a pinwheel or two.

Chapter 4

Getting the Farm Ready

In early May, once we had recovered from our maple sugar comas and burned the grass, we readied the farm for spring. When we had animals, we put them out to pasture. Horses seemed to enjoy being let out and would frolic in the field. The cows just grazed and stared around.

Mother began her spring cleaning. I quickly learned to find something to do outside because she would put me to work if I were hanging around. Dad also spent considerable time "working" outside. There was lots of outside work to keep us busy, so we weren't *just* avoiding cleaning the house.

First, we dealt with the windows—these were wooden, double-hung affairs with a single sheet of glass puttied into each frame. Since these weren't great at keeping the heat in, we had to add a second set of "storm windows" each fall. These were designed to fit the outer window frame, consisting of an upper and lower pane of glass separated by mullions. In spring, we replaced the storm windows with wooden-framed screens.

Replacing the storm windows with screens was onerous. The downstairs windows were no problem, but you needed a long ladder to get to the second storey. When I got older, it was my job to climb the ladder, while Dad held it steady. I retrieved the storm window and then climbed down, grabbed the screen, and scampered back up the ladder to install it.

All in all, there were about eight windows on the second storey.

Another way we had insulated the house for winter was creating a trough of rough boards around the foundation and filling it with sawdust, which was cheap and plentiful. That helped seal any cracks in the masonry and keep cold draughts out—a common trick back then. So, our next big spring task was to clear away all that sawdust and the boards. All told, the windows and foundation were a good couple of days worth of work.

Figure 26. Taking Down Storm Windows

Next was a general yard clean-up and an assessment of our wood supply (which by early May was getting low). Usually, it was too wet for us to take the truck or the tractor into the woods to cut more firewood. Dad's solution was to obtain some slabs from a local mill one way or another.

===

Gett'n Slabs

Slabs are offcuts from squaring up round logs and were often given away (or thrown out). This practice changed in the late fifties, and most mills began charging for slabs. Dad, however, usually knew someone at a mill, and we were able to get a load of slabs for free or at a minimal cost.

Once, on our way to a mill, Dad told me how, years earlier, he and my Uncle Reg were headed back into the deep woods on a Sunday to get (steal, take, liberate) a load of slabs. I guess if something has no value, it isn't technically stealing. Anyway, they were about halfway up an old, backwoods road when they met a truck loaded with slabs coming the other way.

Uncle Reg jumped out of the truck and approached the oncoming vehicle with a "friendly," "What the hell do you think you're doing!" bellowed in an authoritarian voice.

The guys (who were city boys from Moncton) were much taken aback.

"W-we-we were just getting some slabs!" They spluttered.

Reg pursed his lips and stared at them a moment; eyes narrowed.

"You understand this is stealing."

"Well, we thought no one would mind..." Came the uncertain answer.

Reg pondered this for a minute or two. "Tell you what," he said, "give me twenty dollars, and we'll let it pass."

The guys dug around, finding $18, and asked if that would do. Uncle Reg *graciously* allowed that it would. Dad pulled the truck over to let them pass. Dad and Reg then proceeded to seal their load of slabs and headed home, satisfied with a job well done and a profit to boot.

===

Once Dad and I had our load of slabs, we went home, unloaded them, and set up the saw. Handling slabs was a dirty and dangerous business. Slabs are covered in dirt and bark on one side and in splinters (from where they had been rough-sawn) on the other. They were often a bit muddy and (sometimes) had small stones embedded in them. We wore heavy leather gloves to handle them.

When we sawed them into short pieces for the stove or furnace, we had to be extremely careful as the saw spit out sawdust, bark chips, and sometimes stones. You placed the slab on the saw table then adjusted it for the correct cut length. Then, as you rocked the table into the saw, you would look away from the blade to avoid getting hit in the face (or eye) with debris. Inevitably, you would forget and regret it. Luckily, we were never seriously injured, but I did hear stories of serious accidents.

In addition to cutting more wood, there were always repairs required in the spring. One example is the damage caused by ice. Ice would collect on the roof in winter, hanging down in large icicles. Sometimes, it was so bad that we would have to go up and break it off. Often, the damage was caused by ice intruding under the cedar shingles and lifting (or breaking) them. Dad would go up on the roof in early May, fix a few shingles, repair clapboards, and generally spruce up the place.

Meanwhile, Mother had aired out the blankets on the clothesline and scrubbed the entire place from attic to basement in the house. Winter clothing was washed, repaired, and stored. Our spring and summer wardrobes were retrieved, cleaned, and laid out. This was usually followed by a trip to Moncton to visit the Eaton's department store.

===

The Trip to the Big City

When I was small, a trip to Moncton was a spring adventure. Mother would dress me up a bit, and we would head off. We would have lunch at Moncton's *only* Chinese restaurant if I was lucky. Chicken-fried rice and moo goo gai pan were exotic treats in the fifties and sixties. I saw my first movie in a theatre on one of these trips, "Shane." I was totally mesmerised! Naturally, we went to Moncton at other times…but the springtime and the Christmas trips were the big events.

Once I got older, I rebelled at dressing up to go to Moncton. The perfectly rational argument was that "people in Moncton don't dress up every day just because they lived there" got short shrift. The trip to Eaton's was (of course) the main event…even though I always ended up with the predictable sneakers, jeans, and a couple of new shirts.

While my sneakers were being fitted, Dad always recounted how he ran barefoot *all summer* as a boy. Mother was having *none* of that. Oddly, some stores had x-ray machines and took x-rays of your foot to show how well shoes fit. That practice died out quickly, but I did have my feet x-rayed once or twice.

Because we were "church people," I always had to don a new sports coat, white shirt, dress pants, "good shoes," and a tie in order to be considered "dressed up" for church. Since I hated trying on clothes, it was soon over.

===

The Garden

The end of May signalled the beginning of planting season back on the farm. Because Dad wasn't a "real" farmer and had a day job, this only involved planting a large garden. Mom and Dad spent (at least to my young mind) an excessive amount of time discussing what to plant, where to plant it, and the ideal type of beans, potatoes, strawberries, Swiss chard, carrots, parsnips, and a bunch of other stuff.

Once my parents sorted out the plan, we prepared the ground by plowing, harrowing, and fertilizing.[8] Dad would get out the tractor, hitch up the plow, and till the soil. Then we would wait for it to dry out so he could harrow it (loosening the clumps of earth), and dry it out some more. Finally, it was time to apply fertilizer!

We used cow manure; it was plentiful and free. The expression "shovelling the shit" took on real meaning for me. From our manure pile (or a neighbour's), we would shovel a load of fertilizer onto the bed of our trailer. Dad would drive the tractor with the trailer attached to the garden, and we would shovel it onto the garden. Real farmers had a manure spreader—a wagon outfitted with moving chains, which were equipped with fingers that would hurl the manure over the field.

Once we had shovelled the fertilizer onto the garden, we would then use a garden fork to turn the soil and mix it with the manure. This work was hard, tedious, and highly aromatic. Rubber boots with old clothes were a *necessity*, and a bath was mandatory after a day of spreading manure.

Eventually, we would have the garden soil prepared and ready to plant. Energetic discussions occurred about where to place the pole beans, the strawberries, the lettuce, and how many potatoes, turnips, parsnips, and carrots to plant. For the most part, I avoided the garden as much as possible. To this day, I dislike gardening, but I enjoy its fruits.

Even on the small scale of our local garden, planting was considerable work. For each type of seed or plant, you had to know how deep to plant it, how far apart to place the seeds, and whether to immediately water it. Carrots (for example) would be planted close, first. Later, when the seeds sprouted above the soil, they were thinned, with some of the excess transplanted and some just tossed out. I lacked the interest to learn much about it and just did what I was told—usually with poor grace.

By the end of May, the garden had been planted, and then it was time for weeding and tending the garden. Though manure was

---

[8]A harrow is a rough iron frame set with teeth or disks that is pulled behind a tractor (or horse) and is used to loosen and break up the soil.

plentiful and cheap, it wasn't a weed-free fertilizer—cows will chew almost any plant, and the majority of the resultant seeds pass through them. As a result, our garden was a wonderland of weeds. Every day, we spent time weeding. If we neglected the garden for a few days, the weeds would take over the vegetables. I once suggested to my parents that we let the cows eat the garden, collect the manure and next year, our garden would spring up spontaneously. They thought that was funny...I was offended.

However, weeds were not the only problem.

Local critters (such as squirrels, raccoons, rabbits, deer, groundhogs, and most vegetarian animals within two or three miles) regarded our garden as a perfect buffet.

We would devise a way to exclude the beasts, and they would find a way into the feast.

This vegetarian arms race went on all summer! In the first round, Dad put an electric fence around the garden. This was just a couple of strands of wire connected to a battery that ran a current through it (see Figure 27).

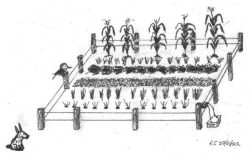

Figure 27. Protecting the Garden with an Electric Fence

Supposedly, this kept the animals away. Of course, they learned to jump over it or burrow beneath it...at least, the smart ones did. The electric fence was some deterrent, but chicken wire mesh fencing worked best. We always put up a scarecrow and a pole (with shiny cans or mirrors that moved and reflected light) to scare away birds. All these efforts worked—to some degree.

Probably the *best* deterrent was turning our dog (Dick) loose. He would be out at night to bark at and chase critters; consequently, many of them moved to a neighbour who didn't have a dog so they could chew on *their* garden undisturbed. We would occasionally patrol the garden in the late evening with a gun, shooting any varmints that ventured nearby. The survivors learned to wait until we had gone to bed.

Somehow, we managed to preserve most of the garden for ourselves. In the fifties and sixties, you didn't have anything fresh until you could pick it from your garden. Today, of course, we have so-called fresh vegetables all year long. Naturally, these "fresh" vegetables were picked green in California or Mexico, then shipped across the country and artificially ripened. I know the vast difference between these poor cousins and naturally fresh vegetables picked from the garden, cooked immediately, and served with a bit of cream or butter. We eagerly anticipated the first carrots, peas, and green beans and enjoyed them immensely.

Then, in late June or early July, there were strawberries. Man, oh man, after eating preserved strawberries all winter, a bowl of fresh strawberries with cream was a real treat.

Even humble tomatoes were anticipated eagerly, and Mother would even pick green tomatoes and fry them to get a start on fresh tomatoes. One thing we lose with the year-round availability of produce is the anticipation of fresh food direct from the garden.

====

Of course, I did more than help with the garden. My school was ongoing. For most of us, early May was torture. We could look outside and see and smell the grass and flowers, but we still had to remain inside and do lessons. Woods or fields surrounded most of the one-room schools we attended, so we played outside at recess and noon hour.

Softball was popular, as was tag, Red Rover, and (sometimes) just running around in the woods. One stupid game someone created was the "Snake Gang." To be a member, you had to hold up a grass snake and let it "kiss" your cheek. Most of the fun was excluding people who were too afraid of snakes to join. Once most everyone joined the gang, the game stopped.

Early spring was also a great time for a walk in the woods.

The first thing you would notice was the smell of pine or spruce. Birch and maple woods were very open in early spring; you could see the leaves beginning to unfurl. Every bush and shrub was starting to open, and the grasses and ferns were just beginning to cover the ground in a bright green. Then, of course, were the birds and squirrels. Red squirrels are aggressive defenders of their territories and would scold you mercilessly when you intruded.

There were some *real* dangers. We were always warned to stay clear of a black bear, mainly if there were cubs. Much more dangerous were moose.

Moose give birth to their calves in April and May. The mothers are very protective of their calves, charging anyone who gets too close. Since an adult moose can weigh up to a thousand pounds (or 450 kilos) and can run up to thirty-five miles per hour, being charged is an experience to avoid. The other problem with moose was that the bull sometimes becomes dangerously aggressive in the spring. Mainly, this was attributed to hunger and being annoyed by an abundance of moose ticks.

Herb Irving was charged by a moose while collecting sap, forcing him to climb a tree. The angry creature lingered for several hours, charging at him every time he tried to descend and escape. Eventually, the moose tired of that game and wandered off. His contention that he climbed the tree wearing snowshoes and carrying two full pails of sap was considered to be an exaggeration.

Despite being warned of these dangers, I never encountered animals larger than a raccoon or a porcupine, but I did run into *hordes* of biting insects.

===

Biting Insects

New Brunswick in general, and Albert County in particular, specialised in biting insects. We had a vast array: blackflies, mosquitoes, moose flies, deer flies, horse flies, and no-see-ums (midges) to round out the blood-sucking crew.[9] Mosquitoes lay eggs in still water; blackflies lay eggs in running water. Backwoods New Brunswick has plenty of both.

First things first, let me be clear: The biting insects of backwoods New Brunswick do *not* use calendars and appear whenever they damn well please. Yes, blackflies are at their worst in May and June but can be found in the deep woods (Oh, joy!) in late August. Mosquitoes are

---

[9] A PhD thesis recorded 108 species of biting insects in the Maritimes. J. D. Lewis (1976), "The biting flies of the Nova Scotia-New Brunswick border region," Doctoral (PhD) thesis, Memorial University of Newfoundland.

rare in early May but not unknown. Deer flies, moose flies, horseflies, and no-see-ums are active *mostly* in June and July; but sometimes last 'til August or even September. All bring their special type of hell.

From personal experience, I know that you can become immune to blackflies and mosquito bites, but the process is uncomfortable, to say the least. All you have to do is get severely bitten two or three times by each species. After that, you won't feel the bites or get itchy bumps.

Deer flies, moose flies, and horse flies are a whole different matter. The first two are subspecies of the horse fly, and all have mostly the same effect. It feels as though someone took a knife and cut out a bit of flesh. It hurts like the devil, bleeds like hell, and can become infected. No way you get used to that. The best protection is a cap, a twill shirt, long pants, heavy socks, and stout shoes—just what you want to be wearing on a hot spring or summer day.

No-see-ums or ("biting midges") are nasty customers. Their bites burn something awful, and you never build an immunity—at least in my experience. Repellants work for all of these to some degree. You have to tough it out for some activities, such as cutting wood or planting in a marshy area.

No one ever wore a short-sleeved shirt, short pants, or sandals in Baltimore. Just no point. Once when my son Alex was small, I took him out for a drive at night to a quarry to see if we could see any deer. We parked and sat in the car with the lights off for a few minutes. When I turned the lights on, the windshield was so covered with mosquitoes, we could hardly see outside! There were no deer, and we absolutely did *not* get out to go looking for them.

===

Mother, the Theological Terrorist

My mother (Gladys) was religious. She took the Bible pretty much literally and had firm ideas about right and wrong. She was an intelligent, energetic, and inquisitive person with deep religious convictions, isolated in a remote, rural farmhouse. For intellectual stimulation, she read the Bible very thoroughly. She also read Bible commentaries from "appropriate" sources. These sources would be from religious folks who believed the Bible is the literal word of God, that evolution is evil, and that most of what we would consider "progressive policies" are the work of the Devil. These were books recommended by radio evangelists or our local minister. I often wonder how her thoughts would have developed if she had been exposed to a broad range of theological philosophies.

Mother had a Bible that belonged to my great-grandfather, the Reverend James Irving, and had some of his concordances and books of commentary. She not only read these carefully; she made notes and also quizzed the local parson whenever he came over for dinner.

In parallel with her fundamentalist beliefs, my mother was a kind person who tried to think the best of everybody and would go out of her way to do what she believed to be right. Part of this came from her upbringing, which also taught tolerance and respect for your neighbours. For example, her father was once approached by the local minister to hold a meeting about community concerns at his farmhouse. He agreed, but when they discussed who to invite, the minister tried to veto one family as they "weren't decent" (in his view). Her father thundered that everyone was welcome under his roof—and that was that!

My mother and father lived that ideal.

Even if she thought your beliefs were wrong, you were welcome in her home if you behaved well. I remember her saying that if you were hosting someone that you disliked, they should be treated so graciously that they would never know your opinion of them.

We didn't get a lot of traffic in Baltimore, but we did get some people showing up at the door. In spring (along with the crocuses and dandelions), travelling salesmen and others began to visit our community.

For example, a French-Canadian guy from Westmoreland County would come around with his truck, selling a variety of fish that my mother would occasionally buy. Then there was the Fuller Brush Man (another travelling salesman), who unsurprisingly sold scrub brushes, hairbrushes, and various household items. In later years, we would also get an Avon lady. Avon is a famous brand of ladies' toiletries that's still in business today. Usually, a neighbour woman would have "Avon parties" at her house, and she would also come around and sell Avon door-to-door, and so on.

The last group of folks that went door-to-door were Jehovah's Witnesses. I don't know much about their theology or philosophy, but I know that recruits are required to go out and try to convert innocent bystanders. When the Jehovah's Witnesses came by, most folks would just say "no thanks" and close the door. A few would invite them in and listen to them; maybe they even got a few converts. But, in our area of Albert County, I doubt that many people were persuaded.

About once every two or three months, typically from May throughout November, Jehovah's Witnesses would knock on our door. Usually, Mother would be busy cooking or cleaning and tended to give them rather a short shrift. In later years (when she was a little less busy), things changed.

The last time Jehovah's Witnesses came by the house was in 1966. I was reading in the living room when we heard a knock on the kitchen door. Mother answered the door, and I heard them tell her who they were before asking her:

"Do you believe in Jesus?"

"I believe in Jesus, but I am not sure you do!" she replied. "You are welcome to come in and tell me what you believe, but I expect you to sit and listen to me afterwards."

They agreed that was fair, so in they came. From the safety of the living room, I could hear that they were excited. So, they trooped in to sit around the kitchen table. Mother (of course) made some tea and put out some squares. After all, they were guests in her home.

I stayed carefully hidden in the living room with my book and just listened. There were three Witnesses (two of them were recruits, the third was an experienced member to guide them). While I couldn't see them directly, I could picture them in cheap black suits, over-starched white shirts, and stringy black ties.

In any event, they gave Mom their standard spiel. I didn't listen very carefully, but my mother did listen carefully and probably took notes as well. She certainly listened to them for a fair spell. They spoke with conviction and energy. Probably my mother was one of the very few people in the last three or four days who would sit down and listen to them.

Eventually, they wound down and said, "Well, how do you feel about that?"

And she replied, "I listened to you. Now, I expect you to listen to me."

She proceeded to go through every major theological point they had made and refuted it based on her understanding of scriptures, quoting chapter and verse from the Bible. Well…they were quite taken aback that she had a counterargument for every argument they had made. Hers were backed up with Bible sources, too. After about twenty minutes of this (amid much coughing, hemming, and shuffling of feet), the senior Jehovah's Witness thanked her very much and hustled his confused charges out the door.

No Jehovah's Witness ever returned to our house again. From friends who knew Jehovah's Witnesses, we heard that we were blacklisted because they were afraid that my mother would turn new converts away from their religion. Who knew that this kindly, little, old lady was a theological terrorist? At least she terrorized three Jehovah's Witnesses that day.

Chapter 5

Summer Abundance

The calendar says summer begins on June 20th or 21st, ending around September 23rd. As a kid, summer started the day school ended (around the end of the third week in June) and lasted until the first day of school in September (typically the first Monday after Labour Day).

Ah, summer! Though I enjoyed school, I *anticipated* summer. As a kid, it seemed endless. In retrospect, it might have seemed that way for my mother, too.

The days were warm (and sometimes hot) by the end of June, though the nights were almost always cool. Usually, there were only about two weeks at the end of July when the nights were hot and humid. The biting insects were terrible in the early morning and evening, but they were not too bothersome during the day if you stayed out of the deep woods.

There was always work to do over the summer. On "the farm," we had two cows, a few chickens, and a large vegetable garden. As a small boy, I remember going down to the barn with my father in the dark of the evening to milk the cows. I was given the honour of carrying the oil lantern! It made scary and flickering shadows, so I kept close to Dad, who chuckled at my apprehension. Once in the barn, Dad pulled up a milking stool, grabbed a pail, and proceeded to milk the cow.

This event was anticipated eagerly by the numerous barn cats, who crowded around Dad as he'd squirt them with a bit of milk. When we finished milking, we trudged back to the house with our brimming pail. Mother took the milk, put it into jugs, and placed them into the icebox (alongside the eggs, butter, and other perishables).

As I got older, things changed, I was expected to do more around the farm. By the time I was seven or eight, we had no farm animals, but there was always wood to cut, things to paint, and lots of weeding.

By the end of June, we were beginning to get produce from the garden. Mother put me to work weeding and helping; but there was still lots of time left to ride my bike on the road or to just wander about with my dog (Dick). Lots of days to read and to self-entertain. For several years, whenever my Aunt Muriel went to summer school to become certified to teach French, Mother returned to the farm where she grew up on the Saint John River to run the house for Uncle Ken. I began my career as a professional strawberry picker and learned about farming. One year, Bea and Garda joined us. Since Garda was only two years older than me, she and I enjoyed working together and hanging out after work, while Bea kept Mother company.

===

Pickin' Berries

Strawberry-picking is hard, hot work. The berry season in New Brunswick lasted through July. As a berry picker on Uncle Ken's farm, I would grab a few empty quart boxes and proceed up a row. Straw paths separated the rows of strawberries which made working on my knees much easier. To pick a berry, you had to twist it or cut the stem with your fingernail. If you squeezed the berry, it would bruise and then rot quickly! You also had to recognize swiftly which were fully ripe and which were not.

The strawberry plants were thick, and you learned to be speedy at your job. You also learned to be good at "topping." When your box was nearly full, you laid the berries on their sides so that the berries came just level with the top of the box. We did this because the quart boxes of berries were loaded into crates, and other crates were piled on top of those. If berries protruded from a box, they would be crushed. In Figure 28, you can see the field and the crates piled at the end of the rows.

Figure 28. Picking Strawberries

If a farmer got a reputation for selling poorly picked or damaged berries, demand fell off sharply. Uncle Ken had a reputation for selling high-quality produce (including berries). He would sell some berries directly from the farm. However, when he had a load, then he would truck them into Saint John. Sometimes as a treat, I got to go with him. Selling direct from the farm was the preferred method as it cut out the intermediaries. The consumer got a better price than at the store, and the farmer got more than the wholesalers paid. This is still true today, when possible, buy directly from the farmer!

Back in the fields, you worked on your knees, row after row, filling boxes. Once each row was completed, you returned to the bottom while picking up boxes to put them in your crate. I was paid twenty cents a box, and might pick fifty boxes on a good day. Since I had free room and board at Uncle Ken's, this wasn't too bad a deal for a kid.

Mother returned home when Aunt Muriel's summer school was finished. When I got a bit older (around thirteen or so), I stayed on the farm for a few summers to help Uncle Ken.

My cousin Philip and I were both on the farm for a few weeks one summer. It was nice to have someone my age around. We were both in our mid-teens and physically fit. We would get up at 6:00 a.m., have a large breakfast, work 'til noon, have a large dinner, then work 'til 6:00 p.m., and have a large supper. After supper (if we had no chores), we would walk down to the cove, swim, and then walk up the road about a mile to a "canteen" (if we had pocket money) for a brick of ice cream. Naturally (around 9:30 p.m. or so), we would eat lunch before bed. Oh, to have the metabolism of a teenager!

Uncle Ken's farm was a mixed dairy and vegetable farm, with some beef and dairy cattle as well. He got up around 5:00 a.m. every morning to milk the cows. In the woodshed (just outside the kitchen door), there was a large cooler for the raw, unpasteurized milk. When the bottles set overnight, the cream would rise to the top. If you were up early and went for a bottle of milk, you were supposed to shake it to mix the cream back in. Naturally, Philip and I would race to get a bottle first and have cream on his cornflakes while the others had skim milk. An *excellent* way to be popular!

Though I love cultivated strawberries, there is a special place in my heart for wild strawberries. If you have never eaten a bowl of wild strawberries and cream, you have missed out. A wild strawberry is about the size of a wild blueberry but has way more flavour than a large, cultivated strawberry. There was a large patch of wild strawberries on the hill behind our house. Mother and I would pick them for ourselves as frequently as possible. Some years, we only got enough for a small bowl each; other years, they grew in abundance. One birthday, Mother made me a wild strawberry shortcake—it was amazing! The problem with wild berries is that it takes a lot of time and effort to pick them because they're so small. The result is worth it, but it's clear why only the cultivated ones are grown commercially.

===

As I reached my teen years, I would pick blueberries at the commercial field up over the hill from our house in Baltimore throughout August.

Picking blueberries was eight to ten hours of backbreaking work, but it paid well. As soon as the dew was off the berries (about 8:00 a.m.), you would take your blueberry rake and head down your assigned row with two empty five-gallon pails.

You raked the blueberry bushes and dumped the berries from the rake into the pail, thus slowly filling the bucket. When both pails were full, you lugged them back to the blower (which removed leaves and other debris) before pouring the cleaned berries into a wooden half-bushel box with your name on it (see Figure 29).

With a thirty-minute lunch break, you repeated the process until about 5:00 p.m. when everyone knocked off for the day. They tallied your volume picked for the day, which was to be paid out at the end of the week.

Then I would head home, usually by walking down the hill through our woods for about a mile. Sometimes, I got a much-appreciated ride both ways with a neighbour.

Figure 29. Blueberry Rake and Half-Bushel of Berries

Blueberry picking lasted about three weeks. However, in the early sixties: I could make about $200 (pretty good money for a kid who'd had no expenses). I used it for clothes and school supplies, though my parents covered most costs. My parents probably spent more on extra food costs than I earned.

===

One summer, when I was about sixteen years old, instead of working on Uncle Ken's farm in July, I had the job of watching the blueberry field: The people who owned the field (some guys from Maine) supplied me with gas and ammunition. I used my dad's truck plus my shotgun (and occasionally a rifle). I had no licence to drive at the time, but as I only had to go on the main road for about a half-mile, no one worried—I learned to drive that summer! The old two-ton truck was a manual stick shift with no synchromesh. That meant that you had to get the RPM to just the right level if you wanted to shift gears. I ground a lot of hamburger that summer!

The deal was this: I would be driving in the field (around 8:00 a.m.), where I stayed until dusk (around 8:30 p.m.). Mom always packed me a good lunch followed (usually) by Dad and Mom bringing me a cold dinner. Although sometimes I would go home, have a quick dinner, and then go back until dark. I had no radio or companion, I just drove around, shooting at crows or any predators. I never hit anything. The crows got used to me and somehow were able to judge just how far to stay away. I tried sneaking up on them through the woods to no avail. They always got away.

Occasionally, I would see someone trying to sneak in and pick berries. Inevitably when I approached, they hurried off. I did hear stories of some guards who had more exciting times.

One time, a well-seasoned field guardian confronted a fellow red-handed with a big pail of blueberries. The thief (who was about fifty feet away) argued rather vehemently about it, so the guardian shot the handle from the pail. Guy tries to have him charged with attempted murder. Later, in the courtroom, the guardian looks at the judge and says,

"Yer Honour, if I'd a wanted to shoot 'im, he'd be dead. I aimed at the pail."

The judge threw out the case. Simpler times!

===

When we had cows, we fed them our hay. Before we had a tractor, Dad borrowed a neighbour's horse to hook to the mower, so he could cut the grass on our property. It usually took two or three days. We waited until it looked as though we would get a few sunny days, and then Dad began to make hay. Once I was old enough to handle a hayfork (probably about six or seven years old), my job was to pile the cut grass into rows or "winnows." Then, after a day or two of drying, we would turn the hay to dry evenly.

Finally, Dad brought out the hay wagon. I would stand on the wagon and keep piling the hay evenly while Dad forked it up off the field. This job was easy when we started, but as the pile of hay got higher, it became hard work to throw it up to the top of the pile. I would try hard to re-pile it to be even and balanced. Dad would sometimes crawl up onto the mound of hay and help if needed (Figure 30).

One day, the pile got away from me, the hay and I slid off the wagon. I was laughing, as it seemed like a great ride. Dad…not so much. Then, of course, he had to fork it all back onto the wagon; where I had to re-pile it, carefully this time.

I enjoyed haying, but it was usually hot work (sunny day, remember) which usually ended with you covered in dust.

Figure 30. Haying Old Style

Eventually, we had a load and Dad would head for the barn. The wagon would stop just inside the barn, and Dad would hitch the horse to the rope and pulleys that raised and lowered the hayfork. In later years, we would have a tractor for that part.

This hayfork would be dropped onto the top of a load of hay by a pulley arrangement. The forks would close, grabbing a large bunch of hay. Then, the horse would walk away from the barn, pulling the rope and raising the bundle of hay to the hayloft. My job was to pull the fork along the track, releasing the hay as I went. I then reset the fork for the next load. (I have provided a reference if anyone wants more information![10]) Then we forked the hay into the back of the loft as fast as we could, and we were ready for the next load. This process was repeated until the upper and lower haylofts were full.

If we were lucky, there would be no rain. If we did get a spell of rain, we would be out turning the cut grass as soon as the rain stopped so it wouldn't get mouldy. The hay needed to be adequately dried out. If "greenish" hay were stored, it could spontaneously generate heat and cause a fire. We always managed, through hard (and sometimes frantic) work, to safely get the hay into the barn. Then, come the fall and winter, the cow (or cows) would have feed.

As the haystack diminished, there was about a fifteen-foot drop from the upper mow to the lower mow. My friends and I would dare each other to jump into the lower mow. When there was still a lot of hay, this was fun. The trick was to figure out when the hay in the

---

[10]Sam Moore, "The Evolution of Haying: Hay barn styles, Mows and Hay Fork Carriers," *Farm Collector*, July 1st, 2001, https://www.farmcollector.com/farm-life/hay-fork-carriers/.

lower mow became too compacted. We determined this by jumping until someone got a bit hurt. Then we usually stopped.

===

Farmin' Ain't for Me

In the summer of 1963, working on Uncle Ken's farm, I decided farming was *not* for me. Folks who have never experienced rural life often romanticise it close to nature; hands in the good earth; blah blah blah....

I do not.

In the mid-seventies, I was an active member of a food co-op in Waterloo, Ontario, until the day that the members (all urban, middle-class kids) voted to get some land and grow vegetables. I knew this was a disaster in the making and dropped out. Sure enough, it went broke a few years later. Why so negative? Well, I knew first-hand how much work there was for scant reward. My Uncle Ken farmed because that was all he knew. He worked hard and did a good job raising fruit, vegetables, beef, and dairy. However, if his sister (my Aunt Muriel) hadn't helped with money from her teaching, the farm would have gone broke.

The last summer I worked on the farm, I was sixteen and stayed on after the strawberries were finished to work for three weeks (before heading back home to pick blueberries). As I mentioned earlier, Uncle Ken got up at about 5:00 a.m. to milk the cows. The other hired hands and I got up around 6:00 a.m., had breakfast, and headed to the fields. In the summer, there were always one or two hired hands, in addition to the occasional nephew.

Because of the hired hands, I met people from all over Europe. In the fifties, there was a program to encourage workers from Europe to come to Canada, if they agreed to work on a farm for several years.[11] I met Horst, a displaced person from Germany. He told us about being forced as a small child to join the Hitler Youth, a fascist version of Boy Scouts. A Dutch couple worked on the farm for a year before settling nearby. I remember going out in the morning and seeing massive wooden shoes by the back door. Finally, a wee lad from

---

[11]Heather Steel, "Where's the Policy? Immigration to New Brunswick, 1945–1971," *Acadiensis* 35, 2 (2006):85, https://journals.lib.unb.ca/index.php/Acadiensis/article/view/10600.

Glasgow worked on the farm for two years. I was fascinated by his accent and got it down rather well. His stories were the source of my initial interest in Scotland.

The farm work was physically demanding and varied. One day, I might spend my time weeding a field by hand. The next day, I might go with Uncle Ken to an island in the middle of the Saint John River to round up some beef cattle, after they had spent the summer roaming free.

The procedure with the free-range cattle was to herd them onto a barge for transport back to the mainland, then onto trucks to be transferred to the "lower farm" for the fall and winter. The cattle (accustomed to being left to their own devices) were a bit wild and dangerous.

When we had finally loaded them onto the barge, Uncle Ken warned me, in no uncertain terms, *not* to walk behind them as they tended to kick. Naturally (as a teenager), I ignored him. What did he know? Not paying much attention, I edged along the north rail of the barge and was standing by the railing when a cow kicked me in the ass. I was lifted up and teetered on the rail, held only by a large belt buckle. Uncle Ken grabbed me, hauling me back on board. He didn't have to say anything. His expression said it all. I had some very well-defined hoof print bruises on my rear for a few days. The bruises to my ego lasted a bit longer, as the topic came up in conversation frequently for two or three weeks.

That wasn't enough to *cement* my dislike of farming, but it pointed it in that direction.

Another incident was transplanting cauliflower with Uncle Ken. The cauliflower field was on an interval—a low, marshy area. Uncle Ken and I each sat on a metal seat on the transplanter, behind a tank of water and with the transplanting device between us. A tractor towed the whole apparatus.

We sat with our legs straight out. On our legs was a sheet of cardboard with a pile of cauliflower plants to be transplanted. Each time the transplanting device clicked, one of us would place a plant in the furrow. The plant would be given a shot of water, and soil would be pushed around it. Subsequently, the other person performed the same process. We carried on in turns until everything was planted.

Not too bad, you think. After all, you are sitting down, and all you need to do is put a plant into the ground. Well, sure…if it weren't for the biting bugs. Many, many biting insects—mainly mosquitoes and midges—converged on us. You were so busy transplanting that you had no time (or hands) free to slap them; you just got bitten. After an hour or two, I was covered with bites, and my legs were stiff. We would do this for eight hours (with a break for lunch) until the field was transplanted, which took a day or two.

This *still* did not convince me to give up on farming…but it pushed me much further down the road.

I *did* enjoy haying. Haying with Uncle Ken was easier than haying with Dad, because Uncle Ken had a bailer that worked—most of the time. Once the grass was mowed, turned over, and dried; we would begin to "bring in" the hay. Uncle Ken drove the tractor pulling the bailer; my cousin and I (or a hired hand) would drive the tractor pulling the wagon for the bales. One or two of us stood on the ground, tossing the bales onto the wagon, while a third person stacked the bales. This was much easier than piling loose hay but still had to be done carefully.

Once the wagon was full, we went to the barn and (using a conveyor) loaded the hay into the haymow at the top of the barn—that was hot, dusty work! When the work was done, we all headed to Mistake Cove for a swim to wash off the dust. Man, oh, man, it felt good! Diving into the salty water (the Saint John is a tidal river) and feeling the tingle as the dust and prickles washed off was total bliss. Half an hour of swimming and we were totally restored.

Overall, haying was a positive experience and did not push me away from farming. But something *else* did.

One day, after a rain, Uncle Ken told me to get a rope on a yearling calf and bring it from the barn to a field nearby. I got the rope on the frisky calf after a bit of a struggle. So, off we went across the barnyard. The barnyard was wet and muddy, sloppy with a mixture of soil and cow shit. About halfway across, the yearling leaped and knocked me to the ground. I held onto the rope, and the damned thing dragged me across the rest of the barnyard on my stomach—fortunately in the right direction. For once, I kept my mouth shut!

When we got to the fence, I regained my feet (if not my dignity) and managed to get the blasted animal into the pasture. Uncle Ken recovered from his rather suspicious coughing fit to comment that I "did the right thing by holding on to the rope." I managed to wash off most of the mud and cow shit in the watering trough, though the others tended to stay well upwind of me for the rest of the day.

That is the day I decided I *never* wanted to be a farmer.

It wasn't all bad. Haying was fun, and in the evenings (somehow), Uncle Ken and Aunt Muriel found time for a social life. I made the mistake of trying to keep up with them once. They completely wore me out after three or four days.

First was the Saturday evening trip to Inch's general store: an old-fashioned general store in every sense of the word. He had butter, nails, olives, work clothes, and most anything else you could imagine. Crackers, pickles, and other stuff were stored in big barrels kept around the store. Shirts and work pants hung from the ceiling. Also, hanging from the ceiling were several old-fashioned tin lanterns. These were circular in shape, featuring a small door for inserting a candle. They were covered with patterns of punctured nail holes that allowed light out as a pretty design. If you imagine an old country store as depicted in the movies, you would be close to my experience.

Typically, there would be about five or six old farmers gathered there on a Saturday night. Each gave their weekly list to Jurd, and while he fussed around preparing their orders, the farmers would gossip about the weather and politics and tell stories.

Thankfully, my almost-getting-kicked-overboard story was only suitable for one evening's entertainment. By the following Saturday, someone else had done something even *more* stupid—and I could slink back to well-deserved obscurity.

I didn't realise it then...but my time at the general store allowed me to participate in a dying social tradition. Jurd's was where political decisions were made, where community information was shared, and where the farmers could host a social gathering.

It was also a place where problems were solved (or sometimes created). A farmer might be having a calving problem; all the others would argue about the problem, until (eventually) a solution would be found.

Forty years later, I read, *The Social Life of Information*,[12] wherein the authors describe how a group of Xerox repairmen would meet for breakfast and discuss repair problems. Theories and approaches were proposed, and (eventually) solutions emerged. These old farmers had created what we, today, would call a "Community of Practice." I know we can replicate this online with Zoom and various discussion forums, but it lacks the personality and aroma of direct face-to-face contact.

Both Uncle Ken and Aunt Muriel were active in local politics and the local church. They would work all day and attend meetings all evening. Typically, one or the other would invite me to join them while they ran an errand in the evening. Sounds innocuous enough. Inevitably, this "simple errand" would involve protracted conversations with several people. God help me, if they started on politics—it would last 'til midnight. After a few days of getting up at 6:00 a.m. and coming home at midnight, I had to beg off any more social activity.

On Sundays, we didn't work—though Uncle Ken still had to milk the cows at 5:00 a.m.—mostly, we rested before heading out for church. My job was to sit beside Uncle Ken and nudge him in the ribs when he began to snore during the sermon.

Working on a farm was a valuable experience, I learned hard work and tenacity; and I developed and retained great respect for farmers. They work extremely hard, take significant risks, and are seriously under-rewarded for their efforts. As a farmer, you are dependent on the weather and the vagaries of the market. Typically, they sell much of their produce to a large distributor, who passes it on to the supermarket or grocery store. The real money is in the distribution chain. Farming is also *dangerous* work. Uncle Ken had a twisted smile. One side of his face was partially paralyzed from being kicked in the head by a cow. In his seventies, he developed ALS (or Lou Gehrig's disease) before passing away soon afterwards. I later learned that such trauma might cause ALS.

So, I ended my farming career knowing what I didn't want to do, but I had no idea what I *did* want to do. Now in my mid-seventies, I have realised that a career is not an endpoint, but an emergent process

---

[12] J. S. Brown, and P. Duguid, *The Social Life of Information* (HBS Publishing, 2000).

that only ends when you expire. But, back home, there still was a garden to tend.

===

Harvesting the Garden

Our carefully planned garden produced a (seemingly never-ending) supply of vegetables and greens. As I've said, we were lucky to have any produce, given the abundance of hungry wildlife, but somehow, we managed. And of course, there were lots of cultivated strawberries from Uncle Ken's farm, along with wild blueberries from our land, plus a few "liberated" from the commercial operation over the hill.

We had new potatoes, cauliflower, Swiss chard, beans and peas, and fresh carrots every night. Mother waited until after the first frost in August to harvest the turnips and parsnips.

Sometime in the sixties, Mother obtained a large freezer and never looked back. She froze strawberries and blueberries, of course. She also froze any leftover vegetables that were freezable such as carrots, parsnips, and turnips. Everything was parboiled and then frozen. More oversized items, like carrots and turnips, were chopped into small pieces first. She would desperately use up any leftover frozen food in the spring to make room for the fresh stuff to come later.

Working in the garden only occupied a small portion of my summer, I got to do some fun stuff!

Whenever I could, I went fishing in the creek below our house. There would be deep pools hosting some large brook trout. I would get my pole, some worms, and head down to the creek for an afternoon of fishing. Sometimes, I even caught a few fish! I'd wander down to the creek, stopping at likely spots, and dangle my worm in the water. Done in a properly languid manner, one could use up a whole afternoon. Since I was "busy," Mother didn't assign chores.

I kept busy that way as often as possible. Naturally, I had to clean the fish before bringing them to Mom. The rule in hunting and fishing was that you clean what you kill. I didn't particularly like trout, but Mother did, so all in all, it worked out. I was busy and out from underfoot, and she got a feed of brook trout.

Riding a Pig

One cloudy summer day, my mother assembled a basket of food for Jim Steeves and tasked me with delivering it—I jumped at the chance. Jim lived by himself in a log cabin up a hollow not far from our house. I always enjoyed an opportunity to visit him, and at nine years old, I felt very grown-up. Off I went, lugging a basket with my mother's admonition not to "make a nuisance of myself" ringing in my ears.

After a fifteen-minute walk, I arrived. The cabin was located on a bit of level ground near a stream. It was a log cabin such as my great-grandfather might have built, with small windows on either side and a covered porch by the front (and only) door. On the north side was a large woodshed; and on the south side (facing the brook), Jim had constructed a pig pen for the biggest hog I had ever seen.

Jim was sitting on the porch smoking his ever-present pipe as I trudged up the path: "Hi Richard. What'cha got there?"

"Well, Mr. Steeves, my mother thought you might like a casserole and an extra pie she whipped up." (No child in the fifties called an adult by their first name.)

"Thanks. Come on in and have a cup of tea with me."

"Thank you, that would be great."

I clambered up the steps onto the porch and entered the cabin. It was one large room smelling of woodsmoke, leather, pipe tobacco, and stale clothing. To my left was a black pot-bellied stove with a large fender, where you could warm your feet on a cold night and a black cast-iron kettle steaming merrily away.

Nearby was a rough table made of small logs, handmade by sawing them in half. It was roughly planed and joined with wooden pegs. A couple of handmade chairs completed the dining ensemble. To my right was a rough wooden bed, covered with old blankets and (what appeared to be) several sheepskins crudely sewn together.

Jim (sorry, Mr. Steeves) grabbed two mostly clean mugs and poured tea, adding heaping teaspoons of sugar. There was no milk. He handed me a mug, stowed Mom's food in a cabinet, and then motioned me to the porch.

We settled into two rough armchairs and began to sip the tea. I figured it'd been boiling on the stove for a long time; it was strong enough to peel paint. But it was sweet, and I didn't dare complain.

"So, Richard, how are things with your Mom and Dad?"

"Oh, about the same, I guess. That is some *big* pig you have there!" I said to make conversation.

"Yaasss, it sure is," he replied.

"It's almost as big as a small horse!" I opined.

"Well, I like to grow them big enough to keep me in pork for the winter. But, if you think it is almost as big as a horse, why don't you see if you can ride it?" Jim said with a gleam in his eye.

I looked the pig over. It was massive, and I accepted the challenge with all the heavy forethought of a typical nine-year-old. Now the pig was clean, and the pen was relatively dry and kempt, so I figured this wouldn't be too bad. Besides, a pig that big…how much can it *really* move?

I took off my light jacket, wandered over to the pen, and regarded the pig. It looked at me disdainfully before resuming rooting around the back of the pen. I clambered over the fence; the pig ignored me. I casually approached; it ignored me.

Piece of cake! I thought.

Once I was beside the pig, I hesitated. It was *VERY* big. On the other hand, it seemed totally immersed in rooting around for something on the ground.

OK, here goes!

I leaped onto the pig's back and (for lack of anything else) grabbed his ears.

Apparently, pigs *don't* like that!

The pig grunted once before taking off around the pen, with me holding onto his ears and desperately trying to stay on his back. He circled the pen twice, squealing like all the devils on Earth were attacking him, then bucked me off. Who the hell knew a pig that big could buck?! I flew over his head, landing square on my back with the wind knocked out of me. The pig, none the worse for wear, snorted disdainfully and returned to his rooting. I lay there for a moment, got up and returned to the porch. Jim was laughing, fit to bust a gut.

"Well, son, *that* is why we don't ride pigs!" He snorted.

The pig, having won the day, stopped rooting long enough to

take a victory lap around the pen.

I swear he was smiling—arrogant sod!

I sat on the porch, sipping my strong, sweet tea and kept quiet.

Later, when mother queried me about the mud stains on my clothes, I mumbled something about tripping on the way to Jim's before skulking off to my room.

I never knew why Jim lived alone in a log cabin. He did have relatives; his brother (Ray Steeves) lived down the road. In the fifties, though, there were a number of eccentrics living off the land. No one seemed to think it to be strange…so neither did I.

Never again did I try to ride a pig.

Chapter 6

Recreation

A discerning reader may have noticed little mention of sports...except for pickup games of softball at school, I had no ready access to any organised sports—no soccer, no baseball, and no hockey. By the time I got to high school, I was eight years behind the other kids and never really caught up. I did learn to skate on Uncle Ken's frozen pond, using my mother's skates. When I was older, Dad created a patch of ice on the interval, and I played around on that.

The only other kid near me was my cousin Garda, who lived about a mile down the road. Still, I managed to keep myself entertained. Summer was a time for me to explore the woods, do some work, or curl up and read whatever I could get my hands on during rainy days. Both Mom and Dad were big readers, so we had many books, plus an extensive collection of National Geographic and the Encyclopedia Americana. Every night, I would take something to bed for reading before I fell asleep. To this day, I still read in bed for thirty minutes or so before sleeping. Both of my parents, despite not being highly educated, were very well read.

Walking in the woods was always a treat. There was something both soothing and fascinating about strolling through the forest and seeing the trees, leaves, and critters. Over several weeks, you would see the growth of plants and flowers. The rustle of the wind in thick leaves sounded much like waves on a shore and the dappled light falling through the canopy created a magical environment.

===

Summer Camp

I went to summer camp several times over the years. The irony of a backwoods boy going to an outdoor camp was lost on me.

The first "camp" experience was at Uncle Ken's when Mom sent me for a week or so to Vacation Bible School at Oak Point Baptist Church. These are three words that should never be in proximity. It wasn't much of a vacation. In my mind, it should've been called "Vacation BIBLE *SCHOOL*." It was held at the local church and was (probably) free or low-cost—we got what we paid for! It wasn't terrible...just dull. Part of the problem was that it was aimed at kids either much younger (or much dumber) than me. We did simple crafts, played a few games, and received an *excessive* amount of Bible instruction of the saccharine variety. Guess they saved the hellfire and brimstone for adults?

Next year, while we were at Uncle Ken's, I went to a Baptist summer camp on Campobello Island near the border with Maine. The island is famous because Franklin D. Roosevelt (the thirty-second president of the United States) had his summer house there. The camp is nowhere near it.[13]

This camp was more like my style! There were games, ponies to ride, swimming, and the occasional excursion on a fishing boat. Of course, in the evening, there were vespers with some preaching and singing around a campfire. Near the end of camp, there were exhortations to be "saved," so I joined the group and was thusly "saved."

The following year I returned...and it was much the same routine. When the evening came for everyone to be saved, I stayed in my bunk (having already been saved). I got my first lesson in group dynamics when the others came back, accosting me aggressively about why I was "missing" from the evening ceremonies.

I calmly explained that I was saved last year, and as far as I knew, it didn't have to be renewed every year. They didn't care and got pissed that I didn't join the group. The next day, one of the counsellors approached me with the same question, and I gave the same answer. He wasn't pleased either. That experience still colours my view of group dynamics.

---

[13] "Campobello Island," *Wikipedia*, https://en.wikipedia.org/wiki/Campobello_Island.

Near the end of camp that year, I was bored because we had the same routine as last year. So, I went for a walk around the island, having spent time in the woods, I knew how to remember landmarks to find my way back. Imagine my surprise when a car full of counsellors pulled up! They hustled me into the car, back to the camp, and straight to the Camp Director...who demanded to know why I had run away.

"I didn't run away," I explained. "I just went for a walk to explore the island."

"You could have got lost or injured!" He thundered.

Though I tried to explain how I was careful to identify landmarks so that I could return *safely*, my explanations fell on deaf ears. At the time, I didn't realise how worried the staff were about losing a kid and how it wasn't good for business. Anyway, we sorted it out and I finished that experience at camp.

My last camp experience was closer to home. Mother found a Baptist camp somewhere outside Moncton and enrolled me for two weeks. It was "Camp Wildwood": founded in 1912 to "give children, youth, and adults the opportunity of an 'Outdoor Adventure' and to develop Christian character."[14] It was located about fifty kilometres northeast of Moncton, and it's still in operation today.

We drove to the bus station in Moncton, where we assembled with the other parents and kids. I wasn't shy, so I immediately started talking to the other kids. Mother, meanwhile, had struck up a conversation with a mousey woman holding the hand of a mousey kid. Since my mother was quiet, she probably picked the quietest person in the room. Nothing would do but that I *must* come over and meet this kid! I sized him up quickly and only spoke to him because Mother wanted me to. Then we all got on the bus and headed off. This looked like fun! There was swimming, canoeing, volleyball, and softball. There were races and crafts; and some minor religious aspects that didn't intrude too much into the fun. The wimpy kid lasted three days, till his mother rescued him.

The mess hall was about standard for any camp—mediocre food but lots of it. Afterwards, we cleaned up the dishes and arranged the mess hall for the next meal. I remember we were required to write

---

[14]"Our Story," *Camp Wildwood*, https://campwildwood.ca/about/our-story/.

home every other day; I managed brief letters and, frankly, wasn't the least bit homesick, though many were. I remember a cabin mate crying each time he wrote home.

The campfires were fun, as was bunking with a bunch of other kids. They had lights out at 10:00 p.m., but we would talk in the dark until we all fell asleep. Usually, by the end of the day, all the sports and running around (in the hot sun, no less) tired us out so we slept well.

====

Camping with the Guys

In high school, a group of us used to go camping and fishing occasionally. We were *not* "glamping": we took sleeping bags, groundsheets, and some plastic to make an awning to keep off the rain. We ate what we caught for the duration of our trip, supplemented by oatmeal, powdered milk, and (until it turned green) baloney.

Four or five of us did these camping excursions about once or twice a year. We were seniors in high school, mostly fit, and looked at our camping as a major adventure.

Two instances stand out.

===

The first major camping expedition was with my friend, Paul (he of maple sugar fame) as well as two other guys (whose names I forget). In the summer of 1964, we went off for three days of fishing on Turner Mountain, about five miles from my home.

We did about as much planning as you would expect from sixteen- and seventeen-year-olds. We had sleeping bags (with groundsheets sewn on the bottom); some sheets of heavy plastic to build shelters; a few eggs, some bacon, powdered milk, instant coffee, oatmeal, and baloney…all packed into a large cooler. We were each armed with hunting knives, matches, a small axe, and fishing gear. Oh, and some mosquito repellant—more on that later.

Dad drove us up an old logging road as far as he could before making it clear that in three days, he would be back at 2:00 p.m.

"Be there or walk home!"

We took his threat seriously, and off we went.

It was about an hour's walk (with all our stuff) to get to the top. Now, Turner Mountain was just a high hill: Albert County has the worn-down mountains of the Appalachian chain that stretches from the southern United States up to Québec. Oddly, the mountain top had numerous brooks and was even swampy in spots. A good place for fishing and an *excellent* breeding ground for mosquitoes and blackflies.

Eventually, we found a relatively level clearing and set up camp. This consisted of throwing our sleeping bags on the ground and starting a fire. We cooked up some eggs and baloney before we set off fishing. The fish were plentiful…and so were the mosquitoes!

After we caught four or five fish each, we went back to camp (as it was getting twilight), cleaned the fish, and started a fire. Figure 31 shows three of us with a large porcupine. I don't remember what we did with it, but I doubt we ate it.

We usually would have jockeyed around the firepit to avoid the smoke. But since smoke dissuaded mosquitoes, we all clustered on the smoky side of the fire. We cooked the cleaned fish in our little aluminum frying pans, with a bit of bacon and that was dinner.

That night, we sat up late, swatting mosquitoes and talking until it got cold enough that the mosquitoes settled down for the night. We all went to bed…but no one got much sleep. Sometime before daylight, a moose crashed through the bushes near the camp.

Figure 31. Camping with the Guys

Everyone jolted awake. We restarted the fire to make instant coffee then sat around until it was light. Afterwards, off we went fishing for an hour or two. In the heat of the day, the mosquitoes backed off, so we napped, laid around, and talked. The rest of the days were much the same. We were running around through the woods, fishing, slapping mosquitoes, cooking fish, and using up our dwindling supplies. The mosquitoes and black flies were horrendous! We had lots of Deet-laden repellants…but Turner Mountain mosquitoes apparently *like* the stuff. It had absolutely zero discernible effect! Ultimately, we just resigned ourselves to getting bitten.

The morning of day three, we were packed and ready by noon. I had some trout in the cooler for Mom and out we walked. Dad showed up at 2:00 p.m., piled us into the car, and then, we headed home (where Paul's dad picked up the other boys). My mother gladly took the fish (fresh caught in the early morning and kept in water in the cooler).

I had so many mosquito bites that you couldn't put a knife blade between them. However, I *was* immune to mosquitoes for the rest of the summer. Mom told me that I went to bed at 4:00 p.m. and slept until supper the next day. Then I got up, ate supper, and went back to bed. Well, in three days, not one of us had had more than about six hours of sleep in total…so it made sense. At the time, I thought it was fun!

Chapter 7

Summer Lessons Learned

I Almost Got Shot

For our last high school excursion, we were much better prepared and we even had tents. This was five guys camping in the woods somewhere, about five or six miles back of Hillsborough. I don't remember the location, except it was off a road…and I believe Paul drove his old jalopy right to our campsite. Again, it was on a "mountain" that had several streams and one large lake.

The first day we just set up camp, did a bit of fishing in the nearby stream, and mostly lay around telling each other how wonderful this was. As we sat around the campfire that evening, one of the five geniuses remembered that there was a private lake nearby, stocked with fish.

Well, what more did we need to know? There was nothing for it, but we had to check it out right then! Fortunately, it was a clear night with a full moon so off we went. After an hour of stumbling around in the woods, we found it: a road leading up a short hill. Over the hill was the cabin, and the lake just beyond it with a dock.

A small rowboat was conspicuously drawn up just beyond the dock. We all lay down on the brow of the hill, seeing lights on in the cabin. Apparently, in the summer, a watchman lived there to protect the fish from poachers. After watching for a few minutes, we slunk back down the road and returned to our campsite.

That night as we sat around the fire, various plans of attack were hatched in our idiot teenage brains. The best scenario was that we should return late one night and steal the boat, row out in the lake, and catch some fish. And believe me, this was the best of all our plans! Of course, there were a few wrinkles: How do we get the boat? Why get the boat at all, rather than fish quietly from the shore as far from the cabin as possible? These quibbles were dismissed as foolish and unimportant.

OK…the next night we would give it a try!

All the next day, we fiddled around the camp. We tried to fish but eventually gave up. We were all so excited about the proposed raid!

Hey, we were teenage boys; common sense was *not* an option. We had a light supper of oatmeal and instant coffee, then hung around our fire until about 10:00 p.m. before we set off.

All went well at first. We quietly skulked along the road to the brow of the hill and flung ourselves prone to scout the area. Everything was dark. There was enough moonlight to see that the rowboat was pulled up beside the cabin. I did suggest, in a *sotto voce*, that it may be chained to a nearby post. This was dismissed as a stupid idea. So, then, who would go "liberate" the boat? After much whispering back and forth, I finally settled the matter myself by just heading down to the cabin.

Having read *The Last of the Mohicans*, I felt my skulking skills were up to par. I quietly walked down the edge of the path, sticking to shadows. When I got near the cabin, I crouched and crab-walked the rest of the way in my best frontier fashion.

All seemed well. I got past the cottage and reached the boat. It was, as I had feared, chained to a post. (Figure 32).

Just then, I heard a SQUEEAAK…

The screen door of the cabin opened. Jumping to my feet, I hurried to the lake, planning to run around the shore to safety. As I reached the lake, I heard the unmistakable sound of a shell being jacked into a pump-

Figure 32: Stealing a Boat to Go Fishing

action shotgun and froze.

The next instant—*KABOOM!*

The watchman fired the shotgun into the air. Clearly, he wasn't trying to shoot me. He fired to motivate me to leave.

It worked!

I ran blindly around the shore of the lake, crashing through the brush, falling into muddy pools, and generally getting scratched up.

Eventually, I made it to the lake's far shore, where I met my friends (who had run the same way through the woods). While I was merely muddy, wet, and scratched; one of my fellow geniuses had managed to twist his ankle. We had to carry him back to our camp.

We had forgotten that, on a still night in the woods, sounds carry. I expect the watchman heard our whispers from that night (or perhaps the night before) and planned a little surprise. It was probably the most excitement he had had for a long time. For us, too!

That night, we were a gloomy and chastened crew. Some of the guys believed that the police would be arriving any minute. Some minor amount of common sense prevailed, and we realised that there was no actual description of us—plus, we were far enough away that we were unlikely to be found. The guy with the sprained ankle was convinced that the watchman would hunt us down and shoot us. I managed to convince him that he could have shot me if he wanted to; instead, he chose to only scare the crap out of me, so nothing to worry about in that regard. One of my less-compassionate companions commented that he was "the only one of us who could not outrun the watchman."

The next day provided another great lesson in group dynamics: It turns out, no one had thought it was a good idea to raid the camp in the first place and each of us only went along because of the other guys. I expect if it'd been successful, the attitudes would have been different. We stayed on until the following day then, fearing some sort of retribution, packed up camp and fled.

There were two good outcomes: We all had a great story to tell our friends in school (though the hero varied with the storyteller). Somehow, when my parents asked about the camping trip, the story of the failed poaching expedition never came up. The other good outcome: I realised I was *not* suited to a life of crime.

Aunt Muriel Teaches Me to Drive

When I was about fifteen or so, Aunt Muriel decided to teach me to drive her car. I had been driving the tractor and the truck around the farm a bit, so I wasn't a total novice. The irony of her trying to teach driving was that she was one of the *worst* drivers in our family.

Until the mid-1920s, the Maritime provinces drove on the left-hand side of the road, like Britain and Australia. They only switched because of pressure from the rest of Canada and the tourist industry. So, on December 1, 1922, New Brunswick switched to driving on the right-hand side of the road. Perhaps that accounts for some of the bad drivers I knew as a kid.[15]

In Ontario, they started requiring driver's licences in the later 1920s and I assume it was roughly the same in the Maritimes. My Dad, Uncle Ken, Aunt Muriel, and Aunt Georgie likely just applied for a driver's licence, paid five dollars, and got it (with no training or test). At least, in Aunt Muriel's case, that seems likely. She drove fast and, to make a sharp turn, she slammed on the brakes and cranked the wheel, signalling optional.

Anyway, she took me out in her car, and we headed down the road. I drove slowly.

After about ten miles or so, we turned around and headed back.

Hey, this is going well! I thought.

Just wait.

I was rolling along at about thirty miles per hour as we approached the farm. Suddenly, Aunt Muriel yelled: "Turn here!"

So, I did. I jammed on the brakes, skidded, and ended up with the nose of the car firmly planted against the front porch.

"Why didn't you slow down?" She screeched.

"Because you didn't tell me to!" I replied with equal volume.

Things deteriorated from there until Uncle Ken arrived to sort us out. He backed the car up, determined the damage was minor, then asked Aunt Muriel in a hectoring tone: "What the heck did you think you were doing?"

The conversation became lively, and I slunk away, totally embarrassed by the incident. After that, I took driving lessons only

---

[15]Julia Wright, "The day New Brunswick switched to driving on the right," *CBC News*, December 1st, 2018, https://www.cbc.ca/news/canada/new-brunswick/new-brunswick-driving-laws-1.4925856.

from my father, who proved to be an excellent teacher.

One other driving incident with my aunts stands out. One summer, Mother, Aunt Georgie, Aunt Muriel, and I took a tour of the Cabot Trail in Cape Breton. The trail is a hilly, winding road, noted for its rugged beauty and quaint towns. It took two days; we stayed overnight in some motel or another. I only vaguely remember the scenery, but I do remember the drive.

Aunt Georgie insisted on driving—thank God! She was a volatile, but good, driver.

Aunt Muriel navigated, and Mother and I were safely ensconced in the back seat. Aunt Georgie seemed to look at speed limits as mere suggestions as we flew up hills and around curves. Aunt Muriel was generous with helpful advice such as "look out!" and "turn here!" offered at loud volume and always at the last minute.

Little is more unnerving to a driver than having someone yell out either of those phrases suddenly. Aunt Georgie expressed her concerns at equal volume, and so it went. I never wanted to take a trip with *either* of them again.

===

Varmints Everywhere

Summer in the country was a time for all God's creatures to be active. There were a lot of them!

One major summer pest was wasps. Paper wasps would build large nests under the eaves of our house. Dad would wait 'til dark when all the wasps were inside the nest. He collected a rag soaked in kerosene and a long pole. He'd put the rag on the end of the stick and stuff it up the hole in the nest; wait about five minutes; then knock the nest down and set the rag alight. This worked about 90% of the time; the remaining 10%, Dad sprinted like an Olympian to the house and slammed the door.

For several summers, raccoons and porcupines were a real nuisance. Fortunately, my dog, Dick, was an expert at killing raccoons. Many mornings we would find a large, dead raccoon on the driveway. Dick was a small-ish border collie with all their smarts. We once saw him tackle a raccoon one evening. It was much larger than him and very aggressive. Dick would run circles around it, feinting an attack until he judged the time was right; then, he moved in quickly and bit its neck, killing it. Over one summer, he killed eight raccoons…eventually, they left us alone. During that mini war, he never got hurt.

His experience with porcupines, however, was quite different. During our porcupine infestation, they gnawed on the wooden sills of the old kitchen and woodshed. It always happened in the middle of the night when all else was quiet: You would be sound asleep and then be jolted awake by *GNAW! GNAW! GNAW!*

Silence. And then, just as you were about to go back to sleep… GNAW! GNAW! GNAW!

After three or four times, I'd hear Dad swear softly and thump downstairs. The screen door would squeak open; there would be a loud BANG! And the gnawing stopped. Dad stomped upstairs, and all was quiet.

Unless another porcupine came by for a feast, and the whole process was repeated.

These incidents went on for several weeks. One morning, we got up, and heard Dick whimpering outside. Going out, we saw that his nose was full of quills. Dad brought him into the house and got a pair of pliers. Porcupine quills are sharp with fine barbs: You cut the end of the quill so they deflate a bit and pull them out with the pliers. Dick quietly sat while Dad ministered to him. When the pain got too much, he would put his paw on Dad's hand, and Dad would stop for a few minutes and then resume. All in all, we pulled about a *dozen* quills from Dick's snout. He recovered in a day or two with no problems. From that day on, he ignored porcupines. Dad once commented, "If a porcupine crawled in his bed, he would just move over!"

Dick liked to chase squirrels and bark at them, just like in the cartoons. Sometimes it looked as though the squirrels were just teasing him. They would run down a tree almost in reach; then, when he charged, they ran back up. This game continued until Dick became tired of it and just lay down and ignored them. At least he got exercise. The barn swallows also liked to dive-bomb him. Unlike the farm cats, he didn't react. He'd just keep going and ignore them.

My Dog, Dick

My dog was named Dick because my mother did not like that popular nickname for Richard, and figured no one would call me Dick if it were already the dog's name. Many years later, Richard Nixon killed off both the proper name and the nickname.

Dick (a black-and-white border collie) was a good dog for an isolated farm. If anyone came by, he would bark vigorously until one of us came out. Once he saw we were friendly with the person, the barking stopped, and they could pet him. He also chased the infrequent cars that came down the dirt road in front of the house. Thankfully, he was agile enough that he was never hit by one. He never caught one, either.

My fondest memory is of him following me down the driveway to wait for the school bus in the morning (Figure 33). In the evening, he would be waiting for me by the mailbox at the end of the driveway.

Mother said that if he were in the house, about fifteen minutes before I'd typically arrive, he would whine to be let out, then down the driveway, he would go.

When I went for a walk in the woods, he would accompany me. Sometimes, though, he would take off into the woods on his own and we wouldn't see him all day.

Usually, at suppertime, he would come home—tired and hungry.

Figure 33. Dick, Waiting for Me at the Mailbox

Eventually, Dick got old, could hardly get around, and was clearly in pain. One day, Dad looked at me and said to me as he held out his gun:

"It's time to end this. I can do this," he went on. "But it is your dog, so it is your responsibility."

"But he's not that bad," I pleaded. Dad put his arm around my shoulder.

"Look at him, son," he murmured softly. "He whimpers every time he moves, and he hardly eats anything. Letting an animal suffer is not the right thing to do."

There were no vet clinics around back then, and even if there were, no one would think to use one for a pet. Vets were for livestock.

Reluctantly, I agreed, picked up the gun, and called to Dick:

"Come, Boy…we are going for a walk."

As I watched him struggle to his feet, I realised that Dad was right.

We headed out, and I grabbed a shovel: No way the varmints would have him for dinner. Dick and I slowly walked into the woods. The more he moved, the easier it got for him…but I could still see that every step caused him pain. Eventually, we were far enough into the woods and sat down to rest under a large spruce.

Dick put his head in my lap, and we just sat there. I remembered all the times we walked in these woods and played outside. I remembered the fights with raccoons and porcupines and the chases with cars. Dick eventually fell asleep. I got up without waking him and, sadly, put a bullet through his brain. He twitched once and lay still. Crying softly, I dug a hole by the spruce and buried him. For several years, I used to visit that spruce and just sit for a bit.

He was my *best friend*.

That summer, I learned that taking care of another living being (and showing love, in general) sometimes involves tough decisions. It was a hard lesson about responsibility but a good one.

Chapter 8

Fall Frenzy

Fall in Baltimore was a hectic time: We had to bring in the last of the garden; preserve fruits and berries; cut wood for the pile; prepare the house for winter; do a bit of hunting for the pot; as well as get ready for Thanksgiving and Christmas. The main contributor to our frenzy was the unpredictability of the weather. It could be nice until November, but we could get a foot of snow in mid-October. Consequently, we tried to get everything done as soon as possible. Also, we wanted to have the work done so we could go hunting in November.

And I, of course, had to go back to school.

===

Doing Up the Fruits and Vegetables

The start of the fall season kicked off in late August. My mother and grandmother would be busy preserving fruits, vegetables, and berries. For me, this mainly consisted of staying out of the way unless I wanted to be put to work, washing an infinite number of mason jars. The whole canning process (or "doing up" as they called it) took about two months of hard work harvesting, cleaning, chopping, blanching, sterilising, and finally, canning.

There always seemed to be a *massive* pot of water boiling while Mother and Grandmother sterilised the jars, covers, and lids. At the same time, they were cutting up apples, blanching strawberries, blueberries, carrots, and peas, as well as generally bustling around the kitchen. God, forbid you got in their way! Dad and I usually found important stuff to do outdoors; while keeping any complaints or observations to ourselves.

Once, I made the mistake of hanging around in the kitchen during the canning process:

"Richard! What are you doing?"

"Uh…nothing."

"Well, I need more beets. Go fill this bushel basket, quick as a bunny. Then, wash them under the pump and bring them here. Now, git!"

"Darn!" said I…and off I went. I had the basket about full when…

"Richard! Where are those beets?"

"Almost done."

"Well, I need them now! Finish up and get them in here. I have a bunch of empty jars, just waiting!"

I hurriedly picked the rest of the beets, washed them, and delivered them…then I tried to escape.

"Not so fast, mister. I need the tops cut off and the beets sliced into quarters. Can you manage that without losing a finger?"

"Guess so…" I replied, reluctantly beginning chopping. After half an hour, I was done, so I slipped outside and stayed there until dinnertime.

Once Mother had sterilised the jars and lids, the blanched fruit or vegetables were put in the jars and topped up with liquid. These bottles were placed in boiling water for a time; then they were removed, their lids were put on, and they were allowed to cool.[16] Once cooled, the caps were checked to ensure they had appropriately sealed before the bottles were stored on shelves in the basement. When, at last, we had a proper freezer, the whole process became more manageable.

Mother canned (or "put up") strawberries, blueberries, raspberries, tomatoes, carrots, cucumbers, and peas. She also spent many hours turning produce into various types of relishes and pickles. Mustard pickles, pickled beets, and chow chow (a condiment made from green tomatoes) were popular, among others.

---

[16] Sharon Peterson, "Water Bath Canning," *Simply Canning*, last updated October 29th, 2021, https://www.simplycanning.com/water-bath-canning/.

My favourite was the canning of mincemeat, which we made with *real* meat, either ground beef or (occasionally) venison. Mother stored it in two-gallon mason jars with a hinged lock-down lid to keep things from oxidising. I used to sneak down to the basement with a spoon and help myself occasionally. I think Mother was onto me, though, as she made comments about how the mincemeat seemed to be settling in the jars.

We also dried beans and apples, too. My grandmother let me help her string Romano beans on rough twine. She used a darning needle to pierce each bean pod, draw the string through it, then go on to the next. I was "allowed" to do this step when I got a bit older. Once we had about a few dozen beans on the string, we cut it and tied the ends together. We used the same process with slices of apples. Then we hung the garlands of beans and apples from nails in the attic, so that they could dry over the winter. The loft was the warmest and driest part of the house, as all the heat migrated upwards. During winter, the dried beans were shelled and cooked with a pork-hock or some ham; while the apples were used for pies.

Our garden also held potatoes, turnips (rutabagas, to be precise), and parsnips, among other root vegetables. We stored them in the cellar, covered in either sand or sawdust; we also kept apples that way. Russets (or "winter apples") were the best type for storing, although they did get quite wrinkly by spring. We picked apples and dug up root vegetables throughout September and into early October.

===

Until I was about six or seven years old, we had chickens for eggs (and occasionally for meat). When Mother decided we would have chicken for dinner, she selected a likely candidate, grabbed it by the neck, and wrung it, effectively killing the chicken. She then proceeded to the chopping block and cut off its head with a singular, well-aimed blow. The chicken would run around the yard in a random pattern for a while until it eventually keeled over…thus the phrase. Mother would dress it by removing its entrails, then dump the chicken into a pot of boiling water for a minute or two. This process allowed her to remove the feathers easily. Eventually, after the carcass was cleaned and prepared, we had fresh chicken for dinner:

no hormones, no special feeds, just delicious, free-range, pan-fried (or stewed) chicken. Mostly, we kept chickens for the eggs: Sometime in the mid-fifties, it became cheaper (and much easier) to get eggs from a neighbour and then eventually from the grocery store, so no more chickens.

I remember Dad telling me that when he was small, they also used to keep geese for eggs, meat, and to sell. One day, my Uncle Reg was teasing the gander, who attacked him and knocked him down. Grandma had to come and rescue him. I am still careful around geese, which can be very aggressive if they have babies. If you doubt me, just try petting a baby Canada Goose.

===

Harvesting Trees

We spent a lot of time in the woods: either hunting, cutting wood for heating, harvesting logs for lumber, collecting sap for maple sugar, or just taking long walks. Mostly, the woods are peaceful places, even if you are working hard within them. They provide resources for living and peace for the soul. If appropriately managed, a forest (or woodlot) can last forever.

Our four hundred acres mainly consisted of a forest with a mix of hardwood and softwood trees. My father, my grandfather, and my great-grandfather before him harvested firewood and softwood lumber there for over a hundred years (between the three of them). One of the saddest days of my life was when I had to sell the farm to get money to cover my mother's living expenses. I sold it to a guy who clear-cut most of the land…we would never have done that. Instead, we harvested the forest, taking only what we needed. I recognise the economics of logging, but I am opposed to clear-cutting.[17]

===

While my father was unemployed for a bit, he cut softwood logs from our woodlot and sold them. On weekends, I helped him harvest the trees.

---

[17]When harvesting trees, only trees that are large enough for logs are cut. In clear-cutting, everything is cut.

First, Dad scouted the land and determined which softwood (mainly spruce and fir) were ready to be cut. These were usually trees of six to eight inches or more in diameter. He then cut a narrow trail with a chainsaw down to the trees from an existing wood road. This trail was a "yard road" for transporting (or yarding) the logs from the cutting site up to the log pile or "brow" near the road. Because our land was so hilly, and we were a small operation, a yarding horse made more sense and was cheaper than a bulldozer or tractor (Figure 34). Dad would cut down a tree; remove the limbs (or "limb it"); and cut it into eight-, ten-, or twelve-foot lengths.

The horse would stand quietly while all this was going on. The horse had a harness that trailed behind him. At the end of the harness were three long chains, each of which ended in a curved spike (called a "dog"). Dad would then drive the dogs into the log and say "Gee up!" to the horse. The yard horse would plod up the trail we had previously cut to the road; where I was waiting to stop it, undog the log, turn the horse around, and send it back down the trail.

Figure 34. Yarding Logs with a Horse

Then, I would use a Peavey[18] and roll the log onto a pile in a flat cleared area (or "brow"), by the road. The horse would return with another log soon after, and I would repeat the process. When Dad felt we had enough logs, he would arrange for a truck to come to the brow, collect the logs, and deliver them to a mill.

The system worked well for a small operator. You didn't have to invest in equipment, and the narrow yarding trails didn't significantly damage the environment. Using a horse allowed us to harvest logs from areas that would be otherwise difficult for something mechanical—such as a tractor or bulldozer—to navigate.

Everything involved in logging is hard work and can be dangerous. Felling trees is no mean art, but there are other dangers. The most significant threat was the chainsaw.

---

[18] A peavey is a lumberman's lever that has a pivoting hooked arm and metal spike at one end. It was invented by Joseph Peavey in Maine in 1858.

Back in the fifties and sixties, chainsaws were heavy, temperamental beasts. Having a two-stroke engine often meant they were hard to start. I still remember how often I exhausted myself by pulling on the starting cable, trying to fire up a recalcitrant chainsaw.

Also, no one I knew wore protective clothing; consequently, severe chainsaw injuries were frequent. These often occurred when a logger was limbing a felled tree: The chainsaw would catch on something and jerk the saw up or down, thus inflicting a severe cut. The other problem was the weight. Early chainsaws were heavy! You were often working over your head, forced to swing it around to make various cuts. Real loggers all had arms like Popeye, with huge shoulders and biceps.

Another danger was handling the logs themselves: When you rolled logs up onto a brow, you had to be careful. If the brow wasn't level or the logs were improperly stacked, they could roll off and crush you. Other dangers existed, too. For example, the chain on a truckload of logs could break (with much of the same effect) if you were too close. And so on.

Experienced woodsmen who had all their fingers and toes were careful people. My father harvested logs for several years, then eventually hired someone to gather them for him. He stipulated that they only harvest trees of a specific size. Once, Dad fired a guy who was cutting pretty much everything. Dad's theory was that at about two or three inches in diameter, a tree was growing fast and, in a few years, would be six to eight inches in diameter, ready for harvesting!

Our land was suited to grow trees above all else. When we cut a patch of hardwood for firewood, softwood trees would grow in their place. When we cut a stand of softwood, hardwood would spring up. Careful management meant an unending supply of hardwood for heating and softwood for sale as lumber. Let's put our small lumbering efforts into the context of the industry.

===

The Lumber Industry in New Brunswick, 1940–1970

Lumbering in New Brunswick was a major industry and changed greatly from the time I was born until I moved to Ontario in 1967. I mention it here because the way lumbering was structured affected how many of us lived and worked. The practice in New Brunswick dates back to the early 1800s, when England used it as a major source of timber for ships. Logs were cut and floated down rivers to mills near the coast, where they were processed.[19]

When I was small, many lumbering operations were unchanged from the early 1900s: Operators still ran lumber camps near major rivers so they could float logs down to mills near the coast. But it wasn't long before lumbering began to slowly mechanize. As late as 1938, manual labour and horses made up 74% of logging costs. As late as 1951, 95% of pulpwood supply in eastern Canada was still being cut manually (using a cross-cut saw or bucksaw). This picture changed rapidly with the introduction of chainsaws. According to the Silversides report, in 1949–1950, less than 1% of pulpwood was cut by chainsaws, but by 1956–1957, that percentage had skyrocketed to 82%. Just three years later, by 1960, 100% of pulpwood was cut by chainsaws.

In addition to chainsaws, the most significant change that affected lumbering was the introduction of bulldozers; and the implementation of small, self-contained sawmills. My uncle Bill (whom you will meet shortly) ran sawmills all over southern New Brunswick.

Using a bulldozer, he could make a road directly to the timber stands so that the logs could be trucked out. He was also able to set up a small mill and process the logs directly on-site, thus increasing profits (since lumber fetched a higher price than raw logs). This also gradually contributed to the disappearance of lumber camps, since many loggers could go home after work.

The lumber industry had also been transformed by logger skidders, which replaced yard horses. There were fewer jobs in the lumber woods, but they paid more. One consequence of extensive mechanization was opening the boreal forests with skidders, chainsaws, and bulldozers. Silversides put it this way in his report, from page 148: "There is no doubt that harvesting forest crops with machines causes more damage to the residual stand and advanced growth than was the case with animal power. No machine has yet been produced to equal the horse for its ability to snake logs out of

---

[19]"All in a Day's Work: Lumbering in New Brunswick," McCord Stewart Museum, *YouTube*, April 28th, 2008, https://www.youtube.com/watch?v=kLlypiw0x_k.

the forest with a minimum of disturbance or damage."[20]

The report notes others who see that clear-cutting operations mandated by extensive mechanization leave little hope for natural regeneration on many sites.

Today, most lumber companies are required to engage in reforestation programs, but there is criticism that these programs tend to favour one or two tree species, leaving the regrown forest open to pests and disease. Still, the forest industry proceeds apace with little indication of slowing down.

While digitization has reduced the demand for newsprint, our use of paper has increased. Some argue that we need to cut out paper altogether.

Digital toilet paper, anyone?[21]

====

Because we were a small timber operation, we cut trees selectively and had no problems with forest regeneration. One problem we did have with our small forest was porcupines. They seemed to love tender, young, softwood trees, taking the time to chew the bark off all the way around—killing the tree. Dad hated them with a passion.

There were a few years when the porcupine population grew out of control. This was partly due to a misguided decision by the New Brunswick government, which put porcupines on the protected species list and forbade killing them. The rationale was that if one were lost in the woods, a porcupine was the only animal that could be killed with a stick, not entirely sure what prompted this decision. At no time did the news ever report hordes of starving hunters lost in the woods, subsisting on porcupines.

Porcupines don't have many natural predators. In Albert County, the most common predator was the bobcat and (possibly) foxes. As you may know (and as my dog learned), the back and sides of a porcupine are covered in hair and quills. Despite popular rumours, they can not throw their quills. Their underside is free of quills, thus,

---

[20] C. Ross Silversides, "Broadaxe to Flying Shear," National Museum of Science and Technology, January 1st, 1997.
[21] The boreal forest (or taiga) is the world's largest biome, covering eight countries. It is typically comprised of both coniferous and broadleaf trees, http://ibfra.org/about-boreal-forests/.

relatively unprotected. A predator who wanted to attack a porcupine would flip it over somehow to attack its underside. Humans (the biggest predators of porcupines) would either shoot them or hit them on the nose with a stick. This drove the nose bone into its brain, killing it instantly. Then all you had to do to eat it was flip it over, and *very carefully* skin it. I was never motivated to give this a try! We were much more concerned about protecting our forest from "quill pigs" than with any government laws protecting porcupines. Whenever we went into the woods, we carried a gun and shot porcupines on sight. After a few years, the population declined to the point where they were not as big a threat, so we were able to relax our war on the "quill pigs" and focus on traditional forest management.

My family wasn't unique in their forest management practices. Most of the locals used the same methods while harvesting firewood and logs for many years.

===

Starting in August and continuing through October, Dad and I spent most Saturdays in the woods, cutting wood for heating and cooking. We needed about twelve cords of wood to see us through the winter. Remember, each cord was four-feet high, four-feet wide and eight-feet long…plus, we did it all by hand. It took a lot of time and hard work to cut and stack that much firewood. Mostly, we cut maple or birch. We preferred rock maple because it burned hot and lasted a long time. We rarely used poplar because it burned quickly and didn't provide as much heat as maple or birch.

Typically, we got up at 6:00 a.m., had an early breakfast, packed a lunch, took our old two-ton truck, and drove up the "back" road to our woodlot. My father had cut a rough road of sorts into the woodlot. We would park, get out the chainsaw and the axes, and get to work (Figure 35).

Felling a tree is a bit more complicated than just cutting it down. Remember, it was in a forest with many other trees around. We would look for a clear place to drop it and look at how the tree was leaning before deciding where to fell it. I would chop a notch in the side where we wanted it to fall; then Dad would cut it down the chainsaw. Sometimes, we would have to give it a push to start it off.

Figure 35. Cutting Firewood

Often a tree would get hung up among other trees, and we would have to work hard to get it down. Sometimes the tree would fall unpredictably, and we would have to step quickly to avoid it.

Once the tree was down, I went to work, limbing it with my axe while Dad picked out another tree. Typically, I would limb it quickly and pull the brush away. Dad would cut the tree in lengths of about seven or eight feet. Then, we piled them on the truck. These trees were usually six to eight inches in diameter and were best manageable as logs. But that was too long for large trees two or three feet in diameter. Those we would cut into pieces, the correct length for the stove or furnace, and sometimes even split them right there. Then on to the next tree, and so it went until lunchtime.

Dad and I would each find a comfortable stump and open our lunch boxes. I'd have a thermos of chocolate milk, a couple of sandwiches, and a square or two. Once, I made the mistake of waving the hand holding the sandwich around. A blue jay, who had been watching me closely, flew down and took it right out of my hand—aggressive, little bastard.

I enjoyed these excursions—the smell of the sawdust and the forest. The work was hard but pleasant, and there was a feeling of accomplishment. Hanging out with my father and learning how to cut wood was also fun. Sometimes he would reminisce about his childhood and share events from his youth. Occasionally, his stories held lessons.

Once, he told me about being in the woods with his brother Reg. It snowed rather heavily as of late, then warmed and froze, so there was a heavy crust on the snow. They were working on a large birch tree. Dad was chopping a notch before felling the tree when a massive chunk of rotten wood fell on his head. It knocked him to the ground and left him dazed. Of course, Uncle Reg just laughed. Had Dad not been wearing a thick woollen hat, the result could've been *much worse* than a slight headache. Lesson learned: Large birch trees often have rotten branches, and you need to look carefully before chopping.

Sometimes Dad referred to a tree bent over with a load of snow as "Fool Killers" (Figure 36). One day when we were eating lunch, I asked him about it:

"Well, sir, you see that birch tree over there?" He said while swallowing a bite of his sandwich. He then pointed at a birch about three-inches around, bent to the ground under a load of snow and ice.

"*That* is a fool killer."

"Why?" I asked him, peering at the tree.

Figure 36. Fool Killer

"Well, that tree is under a lot of strain...and if you chopped into it at the base, the jagged butt would jump straight out. A man standing behind it could get speared through or at least hit awfully hard." He took another swig from his thermos. "Only fools do that."

And that is how I learned forestry. My Dad would have a comment and a story about something, these stories stuck, and I remembered them. Aesop would recognize the technique!

Around 3:00 p.m. or so, we would have the truck bed loaded, and we'd be ready to start heading back home. Once, just as we tried to leave, the truck got stuck in the mud—right down to the axel.

"Dad, how are we going to get out?!" I exclaimed. "We are two miles back in the woods!"

"Well, sir, I guess we will have to think our way out of this one." He pondered for a few minutes while I just fretted. Then, pointing at an eight-foot-long hardwood log (about two inches in diameter: "Richard, drag that long pole over to the truck!"

I dragged it to the truck and poked it underneath the truck, in front of the back wheels. Dad then chained the pole to each back wheel and jumped into the truck: "Now, look sharp! I am going to start the truck and ease it forward. When the pole just rotates to the back of the tires, yell stop!"

As the back wheels rotated, the pole lifted them up, and the truck moved forward about two feet. We repeated the whole procedure four times. Finally, we were out of the mudhole but were both covered in mud—and no towing was required!

When we got home, we would have a cup of tea and a cookie before unloading the wood. If we had a load of long firewood, Dad would set up the wood saw, and we would cut the pieces to the lengths we needed for the woodstove and furnace. Once the logs were cut, we split the wood in half (or quarters) to facilitate drying, handling, and piling. Anything under two inches was usually left intact. We had many large-diameter birch (and rock maple) logs, so there was a lot of splitting.

To split a large chunk of wood with an axe, you either placed it on a flat surface, such as a convenient stump or leaned it against something to wedge it (with another stick or your foot). As I found out one day, the last alternative is dangerous. Typically, I used a splitting axe, swinging it with all my might into the wood to split it. One trick I learned was to give the axe a slight twist *just before* it hit the wood. This avoided burying the axe head in the wood and straining to get it out afterwards. It also made splitting easier.

One Saturday, Dad and I headed back to the woods in late October. There was no snow, but it was cold, around minus six degrees Celsius (or twenty degrees Fahrenheit, if you prefer). Dad had recently bought a new pair of army-surplus leather boots. Since I did not have any warm boots, he let me use them. Good boots were essential in the fall and winter if you worked outdoors all day.

I usually had felt insoles in the boots and wore two pairs of woollen socks. We dressed in long underwear, heavy "Melton cloth" wool pants, a couple of shirts, and heavy wool coats before heading out.

The morning went well: We cut several large trees, and Dad "junked them up" into shorter pieces for the furnace. After lunch, Dad kept cutting trees, and I began splitting. We had a good mix of maple and birch, as I recall. Dad specifically told me: "Be careful with the birch. They don't split straight and tend to spalt off." (Birch was unlike maple, which often had a straight grain and split cleanly.)

All went well for a while. I was about thirteen or fourteen years old, in good shape, and enjoyed the physical experience of swinging the axe. I started with the maple logs and found that by propping them against a large stump, I could split most of them in one blow (if I swung *very* hard).

Then, I moved to the birch logs.

Well, my technique worked on the maple, so I might as well do the same thing on the birch, I thought, forgetting Dad's warning. At first, my technique worked well, and I split some large logs into halves then into quarters.

Then, it happened!

I swung a hard blow at a large birch log, and a piece split off the side. The axe continued through the swing to hit the instep of my left boot, cutting it. My first thought was, *Oh no. I cut Dad's new boot. He is going to be mad!*

So, I kept quiet and started splitting wood again. My foot hurt a bit, but I figured that was just from the blow, so I kept working. Sure enough, around the second or third birch log, another spalt directed the axe blade into the toe of my right boot.

Darn! I thought (as I was a good Baptist at that time and did not swear...then). I examined the new cut and realised I had cut my third toe. I called out: "Dad! I think I cut my foot."

Of course, Dad rushed over to inspect the foot. Yup...it was cut, all right—and it was bleeding freely. Dad found some reasonably clean cloth somewhere and wrapped it tightly. He was just finishing up getting the boot back on when I looked at the first cut I had made on the side of the left boot...and saw blood running out of it.

"Dad? I think I cut the other one, too."

Dad stayed calm, removed the boot, found some more cloth somewhere, and bound that one up. We were heading home. He didn't say anything—didn't have to.

When we got home, Dad said: "I want you to walk in. I don't want to carry you because it would scare your mother."

I hobbled into the house, and Dad explained the situation to Mother. She was a farm girl and had seen many minor injuries, so there was no fuss. She stripped off my boots; washed the cuts with soap; bound them up tightly with gauze; then put some clean socks on me. Her only comment was: "You will be alright."

As I recall, things were quiet in the house that night. If there were comments about safety or anything else, I didn't hear them.

After three or four days of hobbling around, I'd recovered enough to go to school. I had one other misadventure with an axe. At this point, I was about fourteen. It was a January night, and it was snowing heavily. I was upstairs studying; when my dad told me to go and put some wood in the furnace. With all the grace typical of a teenager, I stomped down to the cellar. There were many logs available, but I realised they had to be split. Usually, this was no problem. With a disgruntled teen, a double-bladed axe, and a low ceiling, it *became* a problem. I made an energetic swing at some point...thus causing the axe to hit a joist in the ceiling, bounce down, and gash my head.

As you may know, head wounds bleed profusely.

I ran upstairs, calling for Mom and Dad. Mom quickly grabbed a tea towel and told me to press it on the wound. Somehow, we all got dressed; and Dad drove us the twenty miles to Moncton General Hospital in the midst of a snowstorm. The emergency room doctor gave me twelve stitches, sprayed on some sealant/disinfectant, and sent us home. We got back around midnight.

Did I get a day off school? Nope! I went to school the next day with a note explaining why my homework was not completed. My teacher was more sympathetic than my parents, who thought I was a damn fool.

===

Anyway, let's go back to cutting our winter firewood. We hauled the logs that hadn't been cut up in the woods to the house, where we cut them into shorter lengths using a large circular saw and a rocking table (Figure 37).

The wood saw was a large circular saw blade, powered by a belt from the tractor (or from a small gas engine). The saw blade was attached to a tiltable framework: You would put the log on the frame, move it ahead to the desired length, then tilt the wood into the spinning saw blade.

There were *no safety features*. You kept your hands well back from the saw and looked away from the stream of sawdust as best you could. Once the piece had been cut, you tilted the table back up, removed the sawn piece, and repeated the action. With two people (one sawing and one piling), you could cut up a cord of wood in an hour or so.

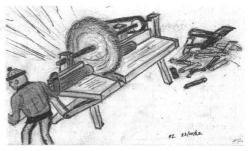

Figure 37. Sawing Firewood

By 6:00 p.m. (about twelve hours after we'd started), we were tired, so we headed back into the house to clean up and get ready for supper. Sometimes, after supper, we would go back out to cut and split wood for another hour or so. If a storm was expected, we worked late into the night to get the wood all cut, split, piled, and covered.

Usually, we let the wood dry for a few weeks before storing it in the woodshed. This required me to load up the wheelbarrow and trundle it into the woodshed, carefully piling up each load. It took quite a while, but it was necessary to get the wood under cover before the snow came. Many people cut their wood a year ahead of time to be well-seasoned (read: dried). We were never that organised.

In addition to hardwood, Dad usually obtained a truckload of softwood "slabs" for kindling and to supplement the other wood we kept. As described previously, slabs were semi-round lengths of logs, the result of running a log through a saw to "square it up." One time, Dad and I drove our truck to a sawmill far back in the woods on Caledonia Mountain. This was an old-time operation: The loggers and sawmill operators lived in a bunkhouse on the property, where they all stayed and were fed at a cookhouse (on-site) until *all* the lumber was cut. After we loaded the truck, Dad and I went into the cookhouse for a snack.

If you were a camp-house cook, you had to produce edible meals in large quantities, at least three times a day. Loggers worked extremely hard and ate accordingly. We arrived between meals, but the cook was accommodating and gave us both mugs of tea (as well as some of the largest slices of molasses cake I'd ever seen).

I was in heaven...but just as I was about to bite into my cake, Dad took a large sip of tea that he had just liberally laced with sugar.

His face contorted, and he ran from the cookhouse and spat out the tea. He kept spitting for a while; I was worried. What if the cook got mad and chased us out before I finished my cake?

It turned out that what Dad *thought* was a bowl of sugar was *actually* a bowl of salt. Turning around, I saw the cook bent over laughing, probably the most fun he'd had all day. Dad got some tea with proper sugar, and I managed to finish my cake. All was well!

===

As you may have gathered from our spring activities, the old farmhouse was solid, but not well insulated. You'll recall the only insulation we had behind the wooden clapboards was birchbark (tarpaper being unavailable when Grandfather built it). As the days grew shorter (and the temperatures colder), it was time to start readying the house for winter: All the window screens we had put up for summer had to be taken down, stored away, and replaced with heavy storm windows. The eight or so windows we had to swap on the second story were tough. While Dad held the long ladder steady up, I went to retrieve a screen; climbed back down to pick up the cumbersome storm window; then lugged it back up the ladder to install it. After that, we'd wrestle the ladder into position at the next window and repeat the process. Normally, we completed this task before it snowed, because climbing a high ladder on a snowy, windy day (with a heavy wooden storm window in tow) was a special treat.

Next, we had to insulate around the foundation by creating a trough and filling it with fresh sawdust (to seal the cracks and stop any draughts, Figure 38).

Figure 38. Insulating the Foundation with Sawdust

All in all, replacing the windows—followed by, of course, insulating the foundation—took us a good three days or so to finish. Once the house was winterized, we turned to more popular activities!

Hunting season (which I recall beginning as early

November) was an exciting time. My Uncle Reg and cousin Basil would be around, as would various friends and neighbours.

Hunting was both a sport as well as an instrumental activity. Ultimately, whatever game we shot was "for the pot." Trophy hunters were regarded with disdain.

I was brought up with guns. After the age of twelve, I hunted with a .22, a 12-gauge shotgun, and my dad's 30-30. In later years, we also had a .38 calibre Webley revolver given to Dad by his friend (Ken Etherly); the Webley was his old RAF officer's pistol. They were supposed to have been destroyed, but most officers just kept them. Ken had served as a pilot in WWII in the pacific region. He once recounted how, one night, at a remote outpost in Burma, he was walking back to quarters from the officer's mess...when he felt a hand brush the insignia on his shoulder. According to Ken, the sentries were all Gurkhas. If they had felt a Japanese badge, the sentry would have cut his throat.

Before I could touch a firearm, the basic rules were drilled into me intensively. First, assume any firearm you pick up is loaded and treat it accordingly: point it at the floor (but not near your foot!); remember to check the chamber (and magazine) to ensure it's not loaded. Second, *NEVER* point a gun at anything you don't intend to shoot. Other than target practice, a firearm is a tool like any other, thus, it's only used to kill animals for the pot—or to shoot varmints (which in our case meant porcupines or the occasional raccoon that raided our garden).

The shotgun was mainly used for partridge, though, I never had fantastic luck hunting partridge. They were hard to shoot because they took off with a loud drumming sound when you got near. This technique was good protection since it tended to cause a predator (me) to freeze for a moment while they escaped. I eventually learned not to freeze, and my mother and I occasionally had several tasty meals. Partridge tastes like the most tender, flavorful chicken you can imagine. They are small, however; so, any average person could eat two (at least). We rarely had more than one each. Fortunately, Dad didn't like them, so Mom and I feasted!

Some people are against hunting-and-killing animals for any reason. I have no problem with that! Although I hunted, I was taught to respect animals.

Yes, we would kill them occasionally for food, be they cows, sheep, chickens, deer, or moose—we had to. For many years, that was a key source of meat. We also killed animals that raided our crops (or chewed up our trees); such as rabbits, raccoons, and porcupines. But we also appreciated their beauty and we never tortured them, or killed them wantonly.

It was also a social norm that you took good care of your farm animals. A few locals violated this rule…and they quickly found themselves universally held in low regard. Some farmers refused to sell animals (of any kind) to these folks. Another social norm was that, if you were going to kill an animal (of any kind), you do it *quickly* and *efficiently*. I heard stories of local hunters trailing a deer for a day because they had wounded it, and they were determined to end its suffering. This was held up (to me) as exemplary behaviour. If you cause a problem, you fix it. The folks I knew respected animals even though they sometimes killed them.

One practice that was universally condemned was "jack lighting" or "jacking." At night, a hunter would shine a bright light around apple trees and fields. If a deer were there, it would stare at the light, and the hunter would shoot at it. First, this was seen as unsporting. Second, there was a good chance that you would *not* cleanly kill the deer but just wound it, making it almost impossible to track in the dark. Third (though this was a minor consideration), it was illegal. Jacking was tolerated only if it were on your property and you desperately needed meat.

Since our house was on a hillside (with plentiful green fields around plus a road nearby), we occasionally heard gunshots nearby at night. Once, a guy came to the house and offered Dad some of the meat. Dad refused, politely, but he refused.

One fall we had a bad time with people stopping on the road and jacking deer across our interval. This flat ground was on the far side of the road from our house, where there were several old apple trees much favoured by deer. I was a teen at that time, and I deplored the practice. So, I found two reflective glass balls (Figure 39), each set in a metal housing, and affixed them to a board, about as far apart as a deer's eyes would be.

Then, I took this rig to the back of the interval and attached it to a tree about 150 yards from the road.

A couple of nights later, we heard a car stop on the road just below and to the southeast of our house. Sure enough: the door slammed, and a bright light played across the interval. Two eyes were seemingly reflected, and—

BANG! BANG! BANG!

I doubt if the shooter would have hit a real deer in the dark anyway. He fired four or five shots, but the eyes didn't move. This was followed by a loud:

"What the *HELL!*" ... Or words to that effect.

He left the vehicle and headed out to see what was up—perhaps I didn't mention that a small brook ran through the interval.

Hard to see in the dark.

SPLASH!

"Oh, what the @*%@, god**@# &**@*##for **&&&!"

Figure 39. Fake Deer Eyes on a Tree

With more swearing, the guy broke off his investigation and left. Guess the word got out that something was amiss near the Irving property, as we had no more late-night jacking that year.

===

The oldest of my Aunt Elsie's children (my cousin David) was an excellent hunter, and he even guided other folks during hunting season. He would often take off for a day or two hunting by himself, frequently coming back with a deer. New Brunswick was (and still is) popular with American hunters who came up every year. Most of these folks were well off, at least compared with the locals. Their gear reflected this fact.

One day David (who eschewed bright red in favour of green pants and jacket—if they can't see me, they can't shoot me) was sitting alongside a trail deep in the woods. Hearing some noise, he looked down the track to see a party of three American hunters—dressed in bright red while carrying guns, knives, axes, water bottles, food, and enough ammo to start a war strolling towards him. On they came, peering left and right until they were abreast of David. When (at last) they spotted him, they all jumped.

"Why aren't you in red?" One of them called out. "I could have shot you!"

David replied: "And I could have shot you, too, about 200 yards down the trail!"

Fortunately, *no one* got shot that day.

===

Hunting changed from the time I was about twelve until I left New Brunswick (in 1967). Improved roads meant that more people ventured into rural areas—not all of them were trained in traditional hunting techniques. One of the first things I learned was never shoot at something unless you could see it *clearly*; and you had some notion of where your bullet would go if you missed, but some folks shot at sounds. It got to the point in Baltimore where you might think twice about going into the woods during hunting season.

The second significant change was the introduction of semi-automatic weapons. These weapons increased the rate of fire, and folks who thought it was okay to shoot at sounds would often empty their clip into the bush. Old-timers (who usually needed only one shot to bring down their prey) disdained trigger-happy hunters.

Finally, I was taught that you never drank alcohol while hunting; that was for the evening in the hunting camp. Sadly, not everyone followed that rule and you'd hear stories of some drunk, shooting at sounds, killing a fellow hunter.

Because of these changes, we were very careful in the woods during hunting season.

Chapter 9

Going Back to School

September was a time of settling into a school routine. Beginning in 1953, at the age of six, I attended one-room country schools that had up to eight grades, consisting of eight to twelve students versus one teacher. I went to three different one-room schools from grade one through grade eight: Osborne Corner, Salem, and Shenstone. Afterwards, I went to Hillsborough Consolidated High School, which was a big change from the one-room schools.

The fall semester was segmented into school, Thanksgiving break, hunting season, and Christmas. School somehow continued through all the external activity. In addition to regular classes, the teacher prepared us for the Thanksgiving break by making paper decorations and by reading related stories to us.

Since we lived in a rural area, some of us would (occasionally) be absent in order to help on the farm for a few days. Hunting season was also a big issue for attendance: younger kids up to about grade seven or eight would be in school; but many high school kids (and some teachers) were off hunting for two weeks in November. Some high schools in New Brunswick even closed during this period!

Christmas was also a big deal in the one-room country schools. (I know it is, technically during winter...but it always felt like part of fall.) The teacher would be responsible for creating the Christmas pageant in which, we sang carols and usually put on a small play or recited poetry. The school would be festooned with colourful paper decorations made by the kids. On the last day of school, parents and relatives would be invited to the performance. There was big anxiety all around, despite how everything received enthusiastic applause. Part of a parent's job, I guess... Thinking back to my own son's performances in grade school in Toronto during the nineties, not that much has changed in forty or fifty years.

Most one-room schools were rectangular one-story buildings that would hold up to twenty students. They typically were a white clapboard wooden structure with a steeply pitched roof and numerous large windows along both long walls. In spring and summer (well, until the end of June), you could open the windows for ventilation. In winter, we would close them, although we still got some ventilation because the windows (typically) didn't fit tightly, countering the heat from the woodstove near the centre of the room.

At the front was a blackboard, nearby was the teacher's desk, with two or three rows of desks along the sides of the room. The school did not have indoor plumbing, so we used outdoor toilets, smelly in the spring and fall and darned cold in the winter. A hand pump somewhere in the school allowed us to wash our hands and get a drink of water. Each desk had a seat and a tablet (or table) built into the front, for writing. A hole for your inkwell would be in the right-hand corner of the desktop, and underneath the seat was a little drawer where you could store your books.

Two of the schools (Osborne Corner and Shenstone) were in clearings cut out of the forest versus the one (Salem) that sat centred in a large, open field.

In Osborne Corner, the main road was just south of the school. North of the road (beside the school), there was a relatively sizeable grassy clearing, a few stumps, and (here and there) a large rock in the woods that surrounded the school. Off to one side were the outhouses and across the road was a small creek; when it froze over in winter, we skated on it.

My first day at school in grade one was eventful. My teacher (Bea Irving, who you'll recall was married to my dad's cousin Omer) was also a good friend of my mother. This arrangement seems great if you're a parent...as a student, less so.

At six years old, it's my very first day. I'm out in the yard with the other kids at recess. There was one kid, by the name of B who I would come to dislike intensely over the years. We were walking around, when he headed into the wooded area just off the playground. He had a screwdriver in his pocket (God knows why), which he put on a stump before climbing a tree and told me not to touch it.

Well…I'm a six-year-old kid. The other guy's up a tree. What am I gonna do? I picked up the screwdriver, waving it around until he slid down the tree, grabbed the screwdriver, and whacked me upside the head.

I was *outraged!* So, not knowing what else to do, I looked and found an empty Coke bottle on the ground. I picked it up and whacked him over the head as hard as I could.

B went in crying to the teacher. She called me over:

"Richard. Did you hit B on the head with a bottle?" She fixed me with a steely glare.

"No!" I replied, all wide-eyed innocence.

She was having none of it and briskly marched me off to the front of the classroom for a strapping. (Capital punishment in school was not only *tolerated*, it was *expected*.) She took the heavy strap of leather and canvas out of her desk to give me two or three little smacks on the hand. The other kids trooped in, and we finished the rest of the day without incident.

When I got home, my mother asked me if anything had happened at school. Again, I said no. Well, she'd already talked to Bea on the phone so, Mother gave me another couple of straps on the hand for lying to her!

===

B was a year older and a grade ahead of me and we were instant rivals. On my first day, he found out that, though I was a bit smaller, I was smarter and quietly aggressive. He was larger, louder, and dumber.

One day, as we played tag, he "tagged" me especially hard and tried to convince the other kids to *always* make me "it." However, I owe him thanks for teaching me a good life lesson. That lunch, he bugged me more than usual.

Mutual taunting became shoving. Then he took a swing at me and missed. I countered with a wild swing that hit his chin, knocking him on his ass while everyone stood around watching.

He was too surprised to yell or cry. After that, he avoided me. I wasn't about to let on that the hit he took was pure luck—no, sirree! What I learned that day, always stand up to bullies. If you win, they will leave you alone. If you lose, they and their henchmen will *still* leave you alone…because they don't want to deal with people who fight back.

Welcome to the *real* world, kid.

===

Most days at school were less eventful than on the first day. Typically, the teacher would give the older students some exercises to do, and then she would sit with the younger students and spend a little more time with them. We started with the alphabet and some numbers. We would then practise drawing our letters while she went on and taught the next class. If you were a smart kid, you finished your homework quickly, then you'd listen in on the lessons that the other kids had. The books we had as readers contained a bunch of simple child-friendly stories, often with a moral message. We did have a "Dick and Jane" reader, among others. The older classes had more ambitious readers as well as history, math, and geography.

In 1959, Bea took a year off to go to "Normal School" in Fredericton, so she could get her teaching certification. Garda stayed at our house, and we started our year in Osborne Corner with a new teacher.

Vicious little devils that we were, we quickly realised that when she turned to face the blackboard, if we all raised our rulers and simultaneously slapped them down on our desks, she would jump in the air, start crying, and run out of the school for a few minutes. She then came back and yelled at us for a few minutes before resuming the lesson. This state of affairs continued for about a month, after which Omer arranged for the two of us to attend Salem school.

Salem was a different experience. The first thing I found out was that Mrs. Colpitts (our teacher) did *not* react positively to me slamming my ruler down when she turned her back. Instead of screaming and running out of the room though, she gave me a detention for causing a disturbance. Mrs. Colpitts was a rarity, in that she had a Ph.D. in English, which allowed her to give us great background on what we read. She also operated a farm, and frequently arrived in school smelling of goat and cow shit. Despite the olfactory distractions, she managed to give us a good grounding in English, history, and math. Mrs. Colpitts also arranged for us to put on a play, and she developed an elaborate Christmas concert.

All in all, grade six in Salem was a *good* year. The only downside to Salem School I remember was my sledding disaster. The school was situated in the middle of a large field. On one side, a steep hill went down to a brook. On snowy days, this was great for sledding—perfect! Of course, I bugged my parents until I got permission to take my sled to school.

On that day, a cold night had produced a great crust on the snow. At noon, off I went. Naturally, other kids wanted a ride. I allowed one of the guys to lay on my back as I sprawled on the sled on my last trip. About halfway down the hill, one of the runners cut through the crust. We flew off the sled. I skidded down the hill on my face, with a kid on top of me. Not too surprisingly, my face was scraped up. The sled came back home and stayed there.

By spring of 1960, Bea had completed her teacher training and received her official certificate. I went with her that fall to Shenstone School for grades seven and eight. Those years were mostly uneventful, but I did meet Loanna, who became a lifelong friend and later, the chief of gerontology at Moncton Hospital.

===

A Day at a One-Room Country School

Wondering what life was like for me during these times? Let's take a walk down memory lane to Tuesday, October 5th, 1954:

"Richard! It is *seven!* Get. *UP!*"

"Okay, OKAY!" I shout back. For early October, it's cold! Reluctantly, I sit up and look around. (*Where are the darned socks?*) I try to find them and put them on before getting out of bed. I check and confirm I can see my breath. No luck with the socks. Swinging my bare feet from the warm bed onto the floor is like stepping on ice cubes. Hopping on one foot, I get one sock on before hunting for the other. By this time, I am shivering a bit. Find the sock; stub my toe on the chamber pot (*Ow! Darn it!*); strip off my blue flannel pyjamas, and jump into my clothes. Thank *God* for home-made wool socks!

"*RICHARD!!*" Mother is sounding decidedly annoyed now.

"Coming, Mother!" I fumble closed the last of my buttons.

Downstairs (as always), my breakfast is magically on the table: scrambled eggs, fried baloney, toast, and chocolate milk. Grandma Maggie is sipping the inevitable cup of tea and getting ready to make bread. Mother is packing my lunch, drinking tea, and feeding Dick—apparently simultaneously.

"Richard, do you have your book bag packed?"

"Yes."

"Did you pack your math homework?"

"Yes."

"Well, here is your lunch!" She said, handing me my Roy Rogers tin lunch pail with the Trigger thermos filled with chocolate milk.

"Did you make peanut butter and strawberry jam sandwiches?"

"Richard, you always want the same thing. Today, you get baloney and cheese and an apple."

"OK! Come on, Dick, it is almost 8 a.m., time to go down to the road."

Dick and I strolled down to the mailbox at the end of the road to wait for Omer to pick me up. After five minutes or so, I see the Ford half-ton come speeding down the road in a cloud of dust. I patted Dick goodbye before I clambered into the cab (with Bea and Garda) for the fifteen-minute drive to Osborne Corner.

"So, Richard, did you finish your homework?" Bea queries.

"Yeah…" I reply, in a desultory way. I didn't like the math assignment, but of course, my mother (who used to be a teacher) made sure I did it.

All four of us talk about the last instalment of Rawhide (a popular radio show of the time), not much else happens. Although, once (on the way to school), we saw a bobcat run across the road, probably the most exciting thing that ever happened on one of those drives! At last, we are there.

Since class didn't start 'til 8:30 a.m., Garda and I went outside to throw a ball around until the other kids arrived. Jim arrived with his brother (Bill) on horseback. Bill was older and just gave Jim a ride to school and then rode back to the farm. They lived on a hardscrabble farm, located up a dirt road about two miles from school. I visited them once and had the second strongest cup of tea I have ever had. They made tea in an old-fashioned way: There was a large metal tea kettle on the stove continually, which just kept gaining tea leaves and water as necessary. When the volume of tea leaves was so great that there was little room left for water, they dumped the kettle and started over. When I had tea, I guess the kettle needed dumping. The tea was so strong and black that even with sugar, it was almost undrinkable. I figured there was about a pound of tea leaves that had been brewing for about a month. It definitely puts some hair on your chest!

Anyway, Jim dismounted to join our impromptu game of catch. As the other kids arrived, they joined in until the teacher rang the big brass bell to summon us to school. (One year later, Jim died when his rather skittish horse was startled by a deer and bucked both him and his brother off, trampling Jim to death.)

We shambled reluctantly into the school and took our seats. These schools were only heated when we were in session, and today the school was pretty cool. A local guy was normally hired to make a fire in the stove, supposedly an hour or so before class. Usually, they showed up. On the days they didn't, the teacher started a fire while we wore our outdoor coats for an hour or two, just until things warmed up. At 8:30 a.m., the lessons began. First, we recited the Lord's Prayer and sang "O' Canada" (the national anthem of Canada which only became official in 1980). Then we got down to work:

"OK, Class!" The classical teacher phrase when calling attention. "The grade eights need to review the history assignment as I will question them in thirty minutes. Grade seven, you have ten minutes to check the "Wreck of the Hesperus,' then I will call on one of you to recite the poem to the class."

She pivoted as she addressed the room in a gentle but authoritative voice. "Grade three, please read the story on page 42 in your reader, and be ready to discuss it when I get to you in an hour. As for grade two, please take out your copybooks and start by copying the lines on page 12 in pencil in your copy books. I will be by shortly to check on your progress. Do *not* use ink until I tell you. OK, let's begin!"

There were just two of us in grade two: me and Karen. We got out our copy books and practised cursive writing in pencil. After two or three times, we relaxed, listening to the other grades work. Most of their stuff was more interesting than what I was doing. I found I could quickly memorise the poems the older students were learning.

We had no ballpoint pens when I was in grade two; so, we used pencils for the first draft. First, we printed the exercise in pencil, then wrote it in cursive. When the teacher deemed our work was satisfactory, we then carefully copied it into our notebooks using ink.

After an hour, Bea came by to review our work, and said the magic words: "After recess, you two are ready to write in ink!"

This task consisted of dipping a straight pen into an inkwell and carefully forming letters on the page. We were only seven years old. Naturally, there were spills, ink blobs, and general mess. Everyone became an expert at removing ink stains from hands, clothing, and books. Penmanship was important and an essential skill, so we practised extensively in special copybooks. I was left-handed (as was my mother), so I learned to write with a backhand slant. A few years later (when Bea had gone off to "Normal School" to get her certification), a new teacher wanted me to curl my left hand to write. Mother was so outraged at this manner of teaching; she taught me to write with my right hand. I've been ambidextrous ever since! When I took engineering at Waterloo, I also became proficient at printing legibly and quickly with boths hands.

One unique thing in cold weather was the thawing of the ink bottles. Naturally, the ink froze solid overnight. We would all place our inkwells on the fender of the stove, like offerings to the God of Warmth. On occasion, someone (by accident, or on purpose) would place their inkwell too close to the stove and "forget" it. An hour or so into class, there would be a *"BANG!"* as the top of the inkwell would bounce off the ceiling atop a small fountain of black ink. It never got old!

Around ten o'clock, we had a twenty-minute recess. The teacher headed off to the outdoor toilet, the girls lined up to use the outhouse, and the boys just took a piss in the woods. Mostly, we played catch and tag, or ran around in the woods (they formed a ragged horseshoe around the school). Then, it was back to our lessons. Karen and I practised writing in ink in our copybooks (under the occasional eye of the teacher) until noon.

Our studies involved much more memorisation than do the

lessons they teach today. We would all have to memorise poems and recite them aloud. We also memorised the alphabet, as well as our times tables. I still know the multiplication table up to twelve! The ability to do mental math (add, subtract, multiply, and divide numbers in your head) is handy and is much neglected today. Recently, a cashier struggled to make change and was amazed when I told her the correct amount without using a calculator. I learned how to memorise my "times" and "goes-in-tas" through my mother's use of flashcards. She would hold up a card with a problem facing me, such as "twelve times eight" or "twenty-four divided by six" with the answer written on the back (facing her). The goal was to memorise them to the point where I could answer correctly, instantaneously.

At noon, the teacher shooed us outside to eat lunch and play. I took my Roy Rogers lunchbox with my thermos filled with chocolate milk; then found a stump (or a large rock) to eat lunch with my friends. Usually, I had peanut butter/strawberry jam or baloney sandwiches; an apple; and a cookie, but today, I had the (ever-popular) fried baloney-and-cheese sandwich.

Then, I loved peanut butter/strawberry jam sandwiches and still do today. We bought Schwartz peanut butter in four-pound metal pails. Mom (who never threw anything out) had quite a collection of these pails over the years. Dad and I used to take one with us into the woods so we could make tea over our campfire. Now, they are collector's items. When I was a student at the New Brunswick Institute of Technology, I took PB-and-J every day. Many years later, a friend told me that he thought I must have been *destitute* if that was all I could afford to eat.

Lunchtime was when we established a hierarchy on the playground. The kids in grades one to three generally played together; then whoever was in grades four and five switched between bossing the younger kids and **being** bossed by the older kids. The older kids in grades six to eight mostly ignored us. Not sure if much has changed today.

After lunch, we had more lessons until about 3:30 p.m. The first lesson was reading. We had the official New Brunswick Second reader. While teaching grade two students to read, the book was filled with stories intended to instruct and improve.

"Richard. Please stand and read today's lesson."

"Yes, Ma'am." I got to my feet and opened the book to page 16. The story was "The Ice Hill," which I began to read in a slightly shaky voice. "The weather had been for some time very cold, and snow lay on the ground more than a foot deep…"

I went on for several paragraphs, and then Teacher asked Karen to read the rest of the story. When she finished, she asked us to write a paragraph telling the story in our own words. While we were doing that, the teacher attended to other students. And so, it went until 3:30 p.m. or so.

Typically, Omer picked us up about a half hour after school ended to drop me off at home. As the truck arrived at the end of our driveway, Dick would be sitting and waiting for me, and we walked to the house together.

"So, Richard, how did your day go?" Quizzed Mother, handing me a glass of chocolate milk and two oatmeal cookies.

"Well, OK, I guess…I read the story 'The Ice Hill,' and practised writing. Tomorrow, I have a math quiz and some homework for tonight."

"No problem. After supper, I'll get out the math flashcards and we can practice. Then you can finish your assignment." Mom said while fussing around the stove to prepare dinner.

After supper, I did homework (with some help from Mom) 'til 9:00 p.m., when we had lunch (a glass of milk and a cookie for me, tea and cookies for Mom and Dad). At about 9:30 p.m., Dad looked at his watch and said: "Time to climb the wooden hill."

And it was off to bed for me.

My father stoked the stoves in the kitchen and parlour, and closed the dampers so they would burn slowly while giving off heat most of the night. Mother would put a hot water bottle in my bed an hour before my bedtime on cold nights. Then I would snuggle into flannel sheets and wool blankets.

====

High School

In 1962, I began attending Hillsborough Consolidated High School (currently called "Caledonia Regional High School"). High school is a big transition for everyone, but it was *huge* for me. Going from a one-room country school with ten kids and one teacher to a large school with two hundred kids and multiple teachers was quite a shock. Also, being in a town with stores and everything was terrific. To get to school, I took two school buses. Fortunately, I wasn't shy and took to school well.

My high school years were mostly uneventful. I was a good student and performed well. I was on the yearbook committee and participated in drama. Since I had no formal training in sports, I lagged behind kids my age and didn't play on many teams. I *did* make a few friends, and we would hang out as much as possible—but this was limited, because I still had to take two buses to get home. The larger bus would pick us up at 3:30 p.m. and drop me at the turn-off for Osborne Corner. By then, Omer Irving had a small school bus and would pick up four or five of us for delivery to Baltimore and beyond).

===

Going to the UN…Sort of

In grade eleven, I wrote an essay in a competitive contest and got to represent Hillsborough Consolidated High School at the Mount Allison Model United Nations (which was held on the Victoria Day weekend, at the end of May). We were picked up at the bus station in Moncton, then bussed to Mount Allison University in Sackville, New Brunswick—about a forty-minute drive east of Moncton, on the border with Nova Scotia. You can imagine the chaos a busload of intelligent, active grade eleven students created.

We were housed in student dorms; and we each received informational packages for the country we each represented: I had Uruguay. We "debated" resolutions and learned about rules of order/debate procedures. Most importantly, we learned about the role of the UN in world affairs (and how, as individuals, we contribute to it).

Though I forget most of the experience, I vividly remember sitting around in a dorm room debating the profound philosophical question: "Would you rather be Red or Dead?" It turns out, we all preferred to be dead rather than a communist. This was our preparation for the talk by the Cuban ambassador. We all tried to trick him into admitting that Communism was wrong and evil. We failed.

The most memorable part of the experience was the opportunity to meet other students from all over the Maritimes and experience a taste of university life. And yes, there *were* girls—though student chaperones kept us separated to some degree, I still managed my first kiss. There were also people of colour, and one or two gay people. It was an eye-opening experience for a backwoods boy.

===

My experience was likely not much different from thousands of other high school students over the last fifty years, so let's skip right over it. One great thing was getting to spend time with Uncle Bill and Aunt Marion, who lived in Hillsborough. When there were special events in the evening (such as a dance or a hockey game), I stayed at their house.

Chapter 10

Fall Stories

Uncle Bill

Uncle Bill and Aunt Marion married later in life and had no children of their own. However, they were very welcoming to me!

Aunt Marion was slight and had the demeanour of a small bird—always fluttering about, keeping her quizzical eye on everything. Uncle Bill (my grandmother's younger brother) was squarely built—not fat, just square—with a calm and very deliberate manner in both speech and movement. He spent his whole life in the woods, running sawmills. He would be hired to walk properties in his later years, estimating how many board feet of lumber they contained.

They had a small, white clapboard bungalow with an enclosed front porch, right on the main street in Hillsborough. After supper, we'd sit on the porch, watch the world go by, and talk. Once, I asked Uncle Bill how he managed to stay healthy so long.

"Two things, I have a bowl of cold oatmeal every night before bed, and I don't waste time getting mad at people," he replied.

Cold oatmeal seemed unattractive…but a calm demeanour made sense. However, just because he didn't get *mad*, didn't imply he didn't get *even*.

At one point, Uncle Bill owned a garage in Hillsborough. In those days (probably the mid-1930s), cars needed continuous repair and Bill was handy with mechanical stuff. As metal parts were not readily available, each garage owner kept a pile of iron bits and pieces behind their shops. When you needed to make a part, you would go and root through the scraps 'til you found a piece that would fit (or from which you could make a part). Yet, Bill had a problem: Guys would hang around the shop, and some of them would go out back and take a leak on (or around) the scrap iron. Bill issued a warning:

"Hey fellas, don't pee on my scrap pile."

They ignored his warnings, but Bill didn't rant and rave. Instead, he went out and hooked a twelve-volt battery to the scrap iron. Sure enough (later that very day), one of the miscreants slipped out the back door. Bill put down his wrench and waited.

AHHHHHHHHHRRRGG!!!

And then silence. The guy did not return for several days, and the desecration stopped.

That's how Bill reacted: He tried to reason. If that didn't work, he didn't yell. He just dealt with it.

I also saw how Bill behaved in the woods. One Sunday, we all went for a walk: my Dad, Uncle Reg, Uncle Bill, and myself. We walked up the hill behind our house, then along the old road into the woods. Bill walked at a steady but slow pace. The rest of us walked briskly and soon left him behind. After twenty minutes or so of hiking uphill, we were winded; we stopped for a rest. Five minutes later, Uncle Bill passed us, going at the same pace with which he started.

"What's the matter boys, can't you keep up?" He taunted light-heartedly as he strolled by.

Well, we walked for another half hour to the blueberry field. Bill beat us there, then turned around and strolled back to the house. He was about seventy-five years old, at the time. When we got home, we were all tired and sweaty...yet Bill was fresh as a cucumber!

Bill lived to be eighty-nine years old. He died while walking across a frozen lake with a chainsaw over his shoulder. Some guys, who were working nearby, saw him fall. By the time they reached him, he was dead. Not a bad way to go, really. Earlier that same year, the Saint John Telegraph Journal (January 17, 1970) printed an article on him entitled the "Grand Old Man of the N.B. Woods." He was a remarkable man, and I was privileged to know him.

We Almost Blow-Up Harold Blake

This story begins around September 1955, when Dad got around to providing us with running water and indoor plumbing. Somehow, he obtained an old road grader. It was a massive, old, yellow monster that sat quietly rusting away in our backyard for years afterwards. Before that, it was crucial to Dad's plans!

Dad used the grader to create a road about five hundred metres up over the hill to a "boiling spring," which bubbled up from a sidehill in the woods. We used it as a well to provide running water. Years ago, a previous settler had dug a hole to install a concrete culvert, so they could collect the water. (An old cellar, up the hill from the spring, was all that remained of their house—we called it the old Liche place.) A heavy metal screen covered the culvert; otherwise, there would be dead squirrels and raccoons in the water. Freshwater continually bubbled up into the container, running away through the maples, and down the hill (towards the spot that, later, would become Dad's sugar camp).

Dad cleared a road and (using the grader's blade set at an angle) managed to dig a trench about three-feet deep. He then ran a three-inch black plastic pipe from the spring to the house, which he then covered with about four-feet of soil to prevent it from freezing in the winter.

Presto! We had an unending supply of fresh water at sixty psi at our home.

The water ran continuously, flowing via a drain down the hill below our house. It was cold and (after being filtered through a mile or two of granite and limestone) tasted great! It was a bit hard, so Mother had to use water softeners in her washing—otherwise, it was perfect.

Dad had previously worked like a maniac to install plumbing for the sink, a full bathroom with a shower, and (of course) a sewer system. He hooked up the water, and away we went. Naturally, there was the usual number of leaks and issues one encounters with plumbing, but he fixed them quickly.

The big problem was the sewer system: Initially, Dad had dug a deep trench lined with gravel and ran the covered sewer pipe into this system. It did *not* work well, so he embarked on installing a septic system—this wasn't an easy task, mind.

Our house was on a sidehill. In that part of Albert County, the bedrock was anywhere from one to four feet below the surface. But, we needed a hole about six-feet deep and six-feet square to install the septic tank properly and get the proper slope. So, we started to dig…and dig…and dig.

Eventually, we ended up with a hole that was about double the width of a grave. The problem was that a large piece of bedrock jutted into the excavation, about two feet below the surface. In effect, we had *half* a hole.

My father wasn't easily deterred…so he decided to dynamite the rock. He never told me exactly how he got his hands on a wooden box of dynamite plus blasting caps. Probably just as well—in any event, there we were with a case of dynamite!

"Well, Richard, I have a job for you!" he proclaimed.

This was *never* good news. He decided to drill holes for the dynamite in the bedrock using a metal rock drill, a stabilising bar, and a heavy sledgehammer (Figure 40).

Figure 40. Breaking Rocks with Dad

Here is how we worked: Dad marked the spot on the rock for six holes. He positioned the rock drill on one hole, with the stabilising bar about halfway up it. I held the bar and kept the drill straight while Dad pounded it with a sledgehammer. Every time he hit the chisel; I felt a shock wave run up my arms. By the end of the day, Dad was dead tired, my arms were numb, and we were both covered in rock dust.

We had drilled three holes about five-feet deep. (This was the same type of equipment that Dad, Omer, and their friend, Ray, had used years earlier. Funny story about them; I'll come back to that later.) Thank God, we had running water and a shower! The next day was a repeat of the first: We managed to finish drilling the remaining three holes. Occasionally, Dad let me swing the sledgehammer while he held the stabilising bar and rested. It was backbreaking work.

By Sunday afternoon, we were all set to blow stuff up: Thankfully, Dad was a careful man. He boarded up the windows that faced the blasting site, leaving a tiny crack in the kitchen window (so that Mother could peer out at our work). Then, it was time for the dynamite!

He showed me how to handle the stuff. Usually, dynamite isn't explosive unless it's hooked to a detonator. However, this was old dynamite...and Dad was concerned that some of the nitroglycerine might have leaked to the bottom of some sticks, thus leading them to become unstable. He showed me how to carefully lift each one and inspect it for oily or wet spots. Those we set aside. Carefully.

In the end, we had about six sticks that Dad figured were in good enough condition.

I learned from my father that you could work safely with dangerous things, if you know what you are doing. If you don't know what to do, leave them alone. My father worked around heavy, dangerous machinery for most of his life and only ever had minor injuries—mainly cuts and scrapes. The sawmill where he ended his work career was (inherently) a dangerous place. Many of the guys there had incurred serious harm—more than a few were missing a finger and several more died from "workplace injuries."

No surprise then that Dad was ever-so-cautious while hooking up the dynamite. We handled the blasting caps gingerly; each one was wired up and carefully inserted into the sticks of dynamite. Dad and I carried the six sticks to the holes, where he carefully placed each one and gently pushed it down with a wooden stick. There were six holes in the rock with wires running out of them into our basement by the time that we finished. Just inside the back door to the basement, Dad had created a firing mechanism consisting of a switch connected to a twelve-volt battery, paired with a set of connectors for the wires.

I, eager to begin, goaded my father: "Come on, Dad! Let's hook her up and blow up some rock!"

"Not so fast!" he demurred.

First, Dad went upstairs and checked with Mother, as they both made sure the windows were adequately covered (in case there was rock debris). Next, he carefully studied and rechecked the wires on the blasting caps, as well the placement of the dynamite. I was dancing from one foot to another with impatience, but he ignored me. Lots of practice, I guess. Finally (after what seemed an *interminable* wait), he hooked up the wires to the ignition device, and we were ready to go. Trembling with excitement, I watched as Dad placed his thumb upon the switch and…

"HAROLD! A man is looking down the hole!" Mother screamed.

To say that Mother's yell "piqued his interest" would be the understatement of the century!

We carefully disconnected the wires before rushing out to our blasting site. There stood Harold Blake (Figure 41) peering down into our hole, with a quizzical expression on his jowled face. Harold Blake was a semi-retired civil servant from Moncton who (sometimes, on weekends) occupied the old, dilapidated Blake house—about a half-mile down the road from our place.

Figure 41: Harold Blake Contemplates Oblivion

When I said, previously, that the nearest neighbour was about a mile away: I was inexact. The old Blake house was falling apart, only occupied by Harold when he came down from Moncton. This weekend he came down and saw us doing *something* in the backyard. Naturally, he came over to look.

"*Harold!*" Dad exclaimed, aghast. "*What* are you *doing?*"

"Well, I wondered what you guys were doing and thought I'd check it out."

Dad raised his eyebrows and gestured towards the hole: "You are staring at six sticks of dynamite wired to explode!"

Harold turned a couple of shades whiter than usual.

"If I had flipped the switch two minutes ago, you would have got a face full of rock slivers!" Dad went on. "Why don't you come into the basement, and we can get on with this?"

So, into the basement, we went…and hooked up the wires (again). Dad double-checked for any more inquisitive neighbours, counted to three,

"FIRE IN THE HOLE!"

The bang was only moderately impressive—more of a loud thump. I wanted to race out and check the damage, but Dad held me back.

"What if some of the dynamite didn't explode right away? Let's wait a bit."

We waited five minutes; Dad sent another electrical signal. We waited another five minutes before we went outside.

Our efforts were successful! An *impressive* amount of shattered rock and rock debris lay scattered around. There were even some shards embedded in the boarding we had put over the windows. Harold alluded to how "it was good that he had not been peering into the hole when the blast went off."

We dug out the hole, installed the septic tank, and hooked up our sewer system two days later. One oddity of our septic tank was that you had a separate system for soapy water, since soap kills the bacteria that fed on the waste. Finally, we entered the modern age of running water, a fully functioning bathroom, and electricity. It was even eco-friendly! The water system used no extra energy, and the septic tank cleaned the wastewater.

I learned how important it is to be careful, and think through whatever you're doing. Who would have thought that someone would have come out of nowhere to stare into a hole full of dynamite? "Check, double-check, and check again" is a good rule. Sometimes, I even follow it!

===

Thanksgiving

Canadian Thanksgiving, which lands on the second Monday of October, was a big event at the farm in Baltimore. The "old homestead" was where all my uncles and aunts were born, so (of course) they congregated there for Thanksgiving. At one point, Uncle Reg, Aunt Cora, and Uncle Bob all lived in Connecticut, so it was a big deal to have them come up. Uncle Reg had a house in Hillsborough where he stayed when he came up; the others stayed with us, or my Uncle Curt (who lived just up the road).

I remember my mother (and grandmother) would start baking about two weeks beforehand.

Cookies and pies featured prominently, as well as cakes and tarts. These were carefully stored, and I was *NOT* allowed to touch them. I got in big trouble once for arguing that I should have access to the cookies because:

"I have to eat here all the time; the guests only have to eat here once."

"*IF YOU TOUCH THE DESSERTS, YOU WILL BE IN BIG TROUBLE MISTER. NOW GIT!*"

About three days before the Big Event, dishes were washed and rewashed, the house was cleaned, and the decorating began. The dining room table was covered with the best table cloth and china on the feast day, and the smell of roasting turkey permeated the house. We'd usually have about ten or twelve people gather when my grandmother was alive. Afterwards, the crowd became smaller.

On the day of, there were piles of food and relatives talking, laughing, and arguing. There were squash, turnips, potatoes, carrots, and parsnips from our garden. Vats of relishes, sauces, and pies galore (pumpkin, squash, and cranberry mainly) adorned the sideboard.

Naturally, there were also stories of past Thanksgivings; and many retellings of events (actual and imagined). I enjoyed hanging out with my cousins, though most were much older than me. Since all of Dad's family was musical, they played the guitar, organ, or fiddle and sang old songs.

On occasion, we had Thanksgiving at my mother's old homestead along the Saint John River. These gatherings were similar, with many uncles and aunts, cousins, and turkey. There was always a turkey.

The history of Thanksgiving in Canada and the United States are a bit different. In the early eighties (when I was working at NYU), I took a few days off in October. Bill H.—one of my students—asked why I was taking off in October. I told him I was driving home for Canadian Thanksgiving. Bill (in true Texan style) queried: "What the *hell* do Canadians have to give thanks for?"

To which I replied, "We give thanks that we are not Americans!" This exchange got me thinking about the holidays and how they developed. Here is what I found:

Thanksgiving in the United States is well known. According to Wikipedia, the first American Thanksgiving was celebrated in October 1621. It lasted three days, gaining an attendance of ninety Wampanoag and fifty-three Pilgrims. In 1870, President Ulysses S. Grant signed a law, making Thanksgiving a federal holiday, falling on the last Thursday of November. In 1942, FDR signed a law making Thanksgiving the fourth Thursday in November.[22]

Thanksgiving in Canada has a different history, though the American tradition influenced it. Our First Nations had a long history of "Thanksgiving Feasts," long before Europeans arrived in North America.

The first European Thanksgiving was recorded by Martin Frobisher, in 1578. Later, on November 14th, 1606, inhabitants of New France under Samuel de Champlain held huge feasts of Thanksgiving between local Mi'kmaq and the French—the Mi'kmaq introduced cranberries to our diet!

In the late 1700s, many of the foods we associate today with Thanksgiving (such as turkey, pumpkins, and squash) were introduced by United Empire Loyalists, who brought their traditions with them. (I'm sure my mother would want me to point out that she always made dressing—not stuffing—to accompany the turkey. Stuffing is cooked *inside* the bird (hence the name), while dressing is cooked separately. The latter method is preferred, since stuffing occasionally contains salmonella.)

===

In Canada, Thanksgiving was declared a national holiday (to be celebrated on November 6th each year) in 1879. Canadian Thanksgiving was declared a national holiday that would fall on the second Monday of October in 1957. This change was based on the fact that the later date tended to conflict with Remembrance Day, November 11 and on the reality that the October date was closer to the actual Canadian harvest season.[23]

So, there you go, Bill, not only is Canadian Thanksgiving *older*

---

[22]"Thanksgiving (United States)," *Wikipedia*, last edited March 7th, 2023, https://en.wikipedia.org/wiki/Thanksgiving_(United_States).
[23]Alison Nagy, "The History of Thanksgiving in Canada," *Canada's History*, October 4th, 2018, https://www.canadashistory.ca/explore/arts-culture-society/the-history-of-thanksgiving-in-canada.

than American Thanksgiving; it more closely follows harvest traditions as well.

You are welcome to help yourself to cranberries.

And we are still thankful that we are not Americans, though I love my American family!

GLADYS IRVING'S OLD-FASHIONED BREAD DRESSING

Ingredients:
- 6 cups bread crumbs (use croutons or make your own—don't use actual store-bought bread crumbs)
- ½ – ¾ cup butter or margarine
- ½ cup chopped onion
- 1 cup chopped celery
- 1 tsp salt
- ¼ tsp pepper
- 1 tsp poultry seasoning
- ½ tsp thyme
- ¼ cup chopped parsley

Directions:
- Put bread crumbs in a large bowl.
- Heat butter in a heavy skillet; add onion and celery and cook stirring gently about 10 minutes.
- Do NOT brown.
- Add all remaining ingredients dry to bread crumbs and toss gently.
- Add butter mixture and toss until well coated/mixed.
- Put in greased casserole or deep dish pie plate.
- Pour 1 cup boiling water over all.
- Place in a 400°F oven for 30 minutes.

Christmas

OK, for the record, Christmas occurs in winter...technically, and (for me) it signifies the end of the school year and the end of fall. The Christmas season was the busiest (and most fun time) of the year. Mother (and Grandmother) bustled about in the kitchen amid the crash of pots and pans. The delectable smells of savoury and sweet wafting through the air and the delicious agony of anticipation of how good it was all going to taste made me drool. The decorations (all those twinkly bulbs and lights) were turning our mundane home into a magical wonderland. The huge Christmas dinner with all the relatives talking and laughing at once was anticipated—as were *presents!*

As the only child of two parents who'd both come from large families, I made out like a bandit at Christmas. At least, it seemed so. My Aunt Georgie (Mom's youngest sister) gave excellent, beautifully wrapped presents. I got lots of stuff from all the aunts and uncles and (of course) my parents.

About a week before Christmas, I would go with my dad into the woods to select a Christmas tree. The ceilings in the old farmhouse were about eight-feet high, so Dad usually got about a seven-foot tree, which we would cut down and haul out ourselves. The tree had to stand in the woodshed for a day or two until the snow melted off, then it was time to install it. Dad made a stand that would hold about a quart of water. He then trimmed an inch or so off the butt of the tree so it could absorb water; we mounted the tree in the stand and dragged it into the house.

The first year, I got a Christmas tree on my own, I made a typical rookie mistake. When in the woods (surrounded by trees), you tend to lose perspective. I came back with a tree about twelve-feet tall. I mentioned to Dad that it was (some hard) to drag back to the house. Dad just laughed and showed me how tall it was. We took off the top seven-feet to use that for our tree. Afterwards, he told me to be more careful, as "that tree would have made a good log in a few years."

Meanwhile, Mother had ventured up to the attic to retrieve boxes of decorations, some of which were very old. Generally, we gathered them up after supper to carefully decorate the tree. My parents were meticulous about where the lights and ornaments were meant to go, and they were insistent that the tinfoil icicles be thoughtfully and evenly placed. I remember disparaging comments about people who just "threw them on the tree." We would then sit around with some ginger ale (Sussex brand, of course) along with some Ganong's chocolates, candy, and nuts while just enjoying it. As a kid, I was entranced by the bubble lights and could watch them for hours—they were *magical*.

At our house, there were no presents under the tree until Christmas Eve. Having had a kid myself, I now know why. Presents that arrived by mail from various relatives were an exception. I remember sneaking in and shaking the ones with my name, guessing what was in them. I never dared open one; the implied consequences were too dire. Late on Christmas Eve, I was usually allowed to open *one* present and a stocking. The stocking always contained some nuts, a small toy, barley candy, and an orange. I think this was a hold-over from when my parents were kids, when barley toys and oranges were rare and treasured items. For me, not so much.

The church was a big deal at Christmas. Larger churches, such as the one in Hillsborough, put on pageants with the children. In our little church, we mostly just had a sermon with lots of Christmas music. I loved the music and endured the sermons.

On the Big Day, I was up early, and I gulped my breakfast. But still had to wait until Grandma Maggie got up. I chaffed and fretted until the old lady finally came downstairs and had breakfast, so we could begin. My mom or dad (and in later years, me) would hand out presents to each person in turn. We would wait respectfully while each person opened their gift, duly admire it, and on to the next person. Somehow, I got the most presents—it all seemed natural at the time.

My favourite gift of all time was a working steam train. It had a gleaming brass engine with a coal car and a carriage that ran on a large oval track. You filled the boiler with water, inserted a solid fuel tablet under it, and lit it. Eventually, the boiler began to steam and away the train went—it even had a steam whistle! I guess it would be outlawed today.

Ah…simpler times.

In the days following Christmas, we would make the rounds of the neighbours. Everyone left their opened presents under their tree (so that they'd be neat and visible for us when we would drop in for tea and cookies to admire their haul). This process of visitation took about a week.

The day after New Year, the tree came down, we put away decorations, and Christmas was over. But before we close this chapter, I must mention our annual Christmas trip to see Uncle Ken and Aunt Muriel on their farm (near Evendale). This trip was about 150 kilometres—or ninety miles; if you prefer—over some rugged roads in winter. We would get up early in the morning and set off. Dad always took the back roads if they were ploughed. We had chains and extra fuel, just in case.

Once we got to Petitcodiac and the Trans-Canada Highway, the driving was easier until we turned off to go to Evendale, so that we could board the ferry across the Saint John River; the road was hilly-and-icy. The hill just before the ferry was extremely steep and slippery. I remember Dad gripping the wheel in grim concentration, as Mother made a point of telling me to "be quiet and not distract him" while he negotiated the treacherous slope. Of course, I was standing up in the back seat right behind him.

Several times each winter, someone would run off the road and sometimes wound up in the river. The river was often frozen so solid that we could eschew the ferry and drive across on the ice. During that time of year, a sixty-mile trip took from two to four hours. My mother told me how they used the frozen river as another highway (Figure 42). Sometimes, they would skate down the river for miles. Farmers would often haul hay across the river from barns using the interval by Mistake Cove.

Figure 42. Crossing the Saint John River on the Ice

Once we got to Uncle Ken's, there was lots of family, food, and most importantly, more presents for me. Yeah! On occasion, my Aunt Elsie and her family would come up from Lorneville, giving me a chance to see my cousins. Lots of *chaos!*

And so, the frenzy of my extended fall ended with a bang. Winter (which, for me, began after the New Year) was much quieter.

Chapter 11

Winter Recuperation

New Year's Eve wasn't a big deal when I was a kid; we had a big meal, and that was about it. At church, the minister would deliver a New Year's sermon focusing on renewal; overcoming the sins of the past; and looking toward a brighter future. I think they got their sermons from a common source and just repeated them each year.

Ah well. Winter—it was a time of renewal. On a farm, the work never stops, but the intensity diminishes considerably in the winter. If you had livestock, they still had to be tended, and there was snow to shovel...*lots* of snow.

And lots of schooling, for me. Our teachers knew that we wouldn't be distracted by planting, weeding, harvesting, and hunting...so they piled on the work. But school wasn't all work, we had lots of play. For one, we had massive snowball fights. We would pick sides: Each side would make a snow fort to duck behind, then the fun began. Mostly, it was good fun. Sometimes a nasty kid (think of someone like B) would wet snowballs and hide them overnight to freeze. They would then pack a bit of soft snow around them and let fly. Usually (after someone came in, crying with a bloody nose), the teacher would find the culprit and punish him—always a "him."

If there were a brook near the school, we would skate on it whenever possible. If there was a hill, we sledded. Winter recess was generally fun, so we were outside as much as possible.

To keep us warm, our mothers would dress us in long wool underwear (itchy), two shirts, a pair of jeans, woollen over-pants, two layers of wool socks stuffed inside rubber boots with felt insoles, and handmade woollen mittens and hats. Home-made wool plaid jackets and sometimes scarves completed our ensemble. We looked like little, fat, plaid snowmen.

===

Winter Social Life

Even though Dad and Uncle Curt had day jobs in Moncton, most folks still farmed and tended to relax a bit in the winter. We had more leisure time and never lacked for entertainment.

Everyone enjoyed board games: Crokinole was a favourite, as was Checkers. The latter was kind of easy once you figured it out. We didn't play cards being Baptists; but we *did* play Scrabble, Monopoly, as well as Snakes and Ladders.

It was common for the family to gather around for a game of Monopoly while listening to the radio. Until television arrived about 1955, the radio was the primary source of news, weather, and entertainment in our house. My mother always had CBC on during the day.

Most every Saturday evening, we would either visit someone or have people over at our own house. These "social" evenings were loosely segregated by sex and age. The women and the young children would congregate in the kitchen. At the same time, the men and older boys would gather in the parlour until the obligatory (and much anticipated) lunch, with lots of tea and cookies and the all-important squares. For that, we all crowded into the kitchen or living room (whichever was larger), where we'd socialise until about 10:00 p.m.—that's about the time when everyone started heading home. Once in a long while, I got to stay up until 11:00 p.m. or 12:00 a.m....but these times were rare.

When I was about eight, I graduated to the parlour with the men. The talk was mostly about local politics, crops, and storytelling. I was privileged to grow up when our oral culture was still strong. This was before television became ubiquitous, and before the roads were improved to the point that travel was reliable and easy. People entertained themselves in much the same way their parents and grandparents had. Almost every house had musical instruments, and people would gather to sing old songs and current favourites.

For me, the fun part was listening to the stories of those present, their fathers, and grandfathers. A good story would be passed down for several generations! Someone who made a witty comment fifty years ago would find it repeated (and probably elaborated) as though they had said it just yesterday. The downside was, if you (or an ancestor) did something stupid, it would be repeated ad nauseam as well.

Typically, there would be Omer (a short and rotund fellow with dark hair, brown eyes, who was quickly fired up). The guys enjoyed yanking his chain. His brother (Herb) was short and lean, with dark hair and eyes. Herb was a great storyteller with a talent for exaggeration. Dad was tall and lean with brown hair and hazel eyes. He enjoyed a good yarn and teasing others. He would sit back with an (ever-present) home-rolled cigarette in his mouth and listen intently to the yarning 'til he could jump in with one of his own.

Most stories were already well known, and if someone were particularly expert at relaying them, they would get a receptive audience. My cousin Basil Turner (a lifelong bachelor) dined out frequently on his ability to tell entertaining stories. Basil was tall and lean with a stooped posture, unkempt long brown hair, and blue eyes; he spoke with a bit of a stutter and lacked education. He probably only kept his studies up 'til grade four or five, given how often he mispronounced words. He also kept an unusual take on the world. He was usually dressed in work clothes and was always dusted with sawdust. Basil was also an expert woodworker…when he felt like it. Everyone admired his turned, inlaid, wooden salad bowls.

He was also teased and made fun of—but, so was everyone. The ability to take and give teasing was a requirement for all of us! Once, I asked Dad about "why he and Uncle Reg referred to hollow-point bullets (known as pneumatic point bullets) as 'stink points.'"

The response I received, "Well, sir," Dad grinned. "Basil calls them, 'P-P-P-P-PeeYOO-matic points,' so we call them 'stink points'!"

Most of the stories revolved around rural life, as you might expect. There were tales of hunting mishaps and successes, lumber camps, and farm incidents. Sadly, I don't remember many of these stories. I *do* remember that when the storyteller was the protagonist, it was invariably about something smart, witty or funny that *they* had done; when it was about something stupid, it was about what *others* had done.

Most of the stories were about the level of the Three Stooges; physical humour dominated.

Here are a few that I can recall.

===

Winter Memories

Dad often told me how he (and his brothers) would like to tease Uncle Reg. Mostly, this was because Reg had a temper as hot as his flaming red hair.

For example, at Christmas, Dad (along with one or two of his older brothers) would take a turnip, put it in a nice box, wrap it well, put Reg's name on it, and place it under the tree. They got great pleasure from watching Reg shake the present and wonder what it was, looking on with even *greater* delight as he opened it to find the turnip. He knew who the culprits were, and (I'm sure) he exacted his revenge…but, Dad was curiously silent about *that* part of the story.

Another time, when Dad was around eight or nine, he saw Reg sleeping in a rocking chair in the kitchen. Quietly, he tied Reg's braces (you might call them suspenders) to the back of the rocking chair, then walked around in front and slapped him in the face. Reg bounded awake and took after my father, who ran through a doorway. Reg's braces and the rocking chair held him in the portal, while Dad escaped safely. I wish I had heard Uncle Reg's version of that one!

There was another story often retold to me from my grandfather, Sandy. One day, Grandfather Sandy was working with a neighbour, George, in the middle of the winter. There was a hard crust on the snow that day as they walked up a hillside to cut some wood. A little while later, George had to "take a dump," as they used to say. Well…he lowered his drawers and had just squatted down when his feet slipped on the crust—and down the hill, he slid: boots in the air and bare arse!

In grandfather's words, "It was blood and hair all the way to the crick!"

Definitely "Three Stooges" material.

Dad also loved to tell of a prank that he (with his cousin Omer) played on their neighbour, Ray Steeves. They were working for Ray, breaking up large rocks using a steel maul, a chisel, and a long holder for the chisel. (The same set-up Dad and I used years later when we almost blew-up Harold Blake, see Figure 40.) One of them placed the chisel in a hole with a long rod to steady it while someone else (in this case, Ray) hit it with a sledgehammer.

Omer was holding the rod, and Ray was swinging away with all his might. Dad walked up quietly behind him and timed it so his hand just grazed the sledgehammer's face just as Ray brought it back over his shoulder. *SMACK!* Dad immediately fell to the ground, pretending to be unconscious. Ray spun around and started freaking out because he thought he had killed him. After a minute, Dad jumped up, all okay. Ray was *not* impressed, though Dad and Omer thought this a great joke.

Three Stooges all the way!

===

My mother and her friends had their stories, too…like how there was a lady at a church social who "put on airs." Now, most of the ladies at Oak Point Baptist Church on the Saint John River were "salt of the earth" sorts: friendly, caring, religious, and immensely practical. They all had good manners, but little use for folks who were overly fussy or prissy.

This one lady stood out because she was fastidious to the *extreme*. When she was loading her plate and came to the beans, she primly asked for: "Just a tiny spoonful, please."

She repeated this request at all the food stations, ending with a sparse plate. As she ate the beans, she cut each one in half and ate each half separately! This was just too dainty for the locals, who all worked hard and had good appetites. When the dinner was over, some guys looked through the basement window of the church: Lo and behold! If it wasn't "Miss Priss," face practically buried, attacking the bean crock with a soup ladle.

Their gleeful shouts of "Just a spoonful, please!" were *not* well received. The lady fled, blushing as red as her stolen beans.

Ah, how I miss the stories. So many of them are lost now to the years and my fading memories. Our oral tradition slowly declined with the advent of television. As the sixties dawned, people tended to cluster around "the box" and talk less. In the 1990s, I spent some time in Saint John's, Newfoundland, where the local oral tradition was still alive and well. May it live forever.

===

Fun in the Snow

Winters in New Brunswick in the fifties and sixties involved lots of snow. Our house was on a hill with a moderately long driveway. In the winter, Dad and I would spend hours shovelling it. At some point, I remember Dad parking in our old barn across the road to minimise shovelling. Later (probably because the barn had deteriorated and became unsafe), he parked by the house at least until we tore down the barn and built an oversized garage.

When I speak of snow, I mean five feet *or more* around the whole house. Partly this was normal drifting, and part was just heavy snowfalls. To shovel the driveway, Dad first used a crosscut saw (with one of the two handles removed) to cut the snow into blocks (Figure 43).

Figure 43. Shovelling Snow

We would then use square, flat-bladed shovels to cut blocks of ice loose and throw them to the side. It usually took the two of us about half a day to complete. By then, the snow plough would come by and fill the end of the driveway—so we would spend another two hours shovelling that out.

By mid-winter, the sides of the driveway would be piled so high with snow on either side that it was like driving up a tunnel.

Since the snow would pile up around the house and woodshed, I had fun making snow tunnels and generally digging around. Once, I dug a particularly ambitious tunnel alongside the woodshed and was *quite upset* when Dad ruined it by falling through the roof. He was singularly unsympathetic, though I remember my mother laughing from the kitchen window.

When I was about eight, Dad and I (mainly Dad) made skis and snowshoes one winter. We began by finding some ash—Dad must have cut it the previous summer, as I remember he had several pieces of ash stored in the basement drying. Ash was preferred for both skis and snowshoes; because it was a strong, straight-grained wood that was relatively easy to steam and bend to shape.

First, we cut the eight-foot lengths of semi-dried ash to size. Dad rip-sawed the ash to boards about three inches wide and one-and-a-half-inches thick for the skis. He made four boards like this for two pairs of skis, with plenty of ash in reserve for more as needed.

He split the remaining wood into strips about one-inch square and eight-feet long for the snowshoes. Dad planed the skis smooth on the bottom to about one inch, then rounded one end of each board to make tips. Then, he steamed them overnight in a steamer cabinet that he'd custom built. The following day, Dad bent the tips of the skis, before letting them dry for a day or two in a home-made jig (Figure 44).

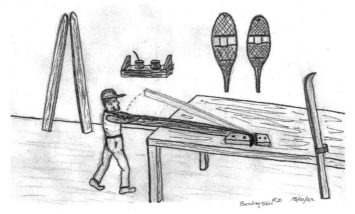

Figure 44. Bending the Skis

Once they were dry, he tacked a leather strap to each ski, we waxed the bottoms, and they were ready to go! We had no fancy bindings or ski poles; we just shoved our rubber boots into the straps.

So, Dad taught me to ski. We trudged up the hill behind the house, Dad set a track down the hill, and I would try to follow. It took a few attempts; but I was soon able to follow it. The track became well set and polished after a few passes. Fortunately, the hill ended in a flat spot before the road, so there was plenty of space to slow down at the bottom. After that, I would spend hours just skiing down and trudging back up! One day, Dad asked if I would like to try a ski jump. I was eight years old. *You bet I would!*

He got an old oil drum and laid it sideways, about three-quarters of the way down the hill. Then, he found an old door and placed it lengthwise on the drum—aligned with the tracks we had made. The next step was to cover it with about two feet of well-packed snow.

Voilà! The ski jump was ready.

The first five or six attempts did not go well. I flew off in all directions, rolling head-over-heels repeatedly. Since they had no secure bindings, my skis propellered every which way, and I had to retrieve them each time. Amazing how far they could travel on their own! Eventually, I learned to lean forward just the right amount and bend my knees as I touched down to stay on my feet. This was fun! Again, many hours up and down the hill.

Dad sometimes went out, and he was actually pretty good at the jump! Mom, however, wasn't interested in skiing or jumping.

One morning, I went out to find that the track had iced up. Wow. Did I have a fast run or what! I came off that jump the highest I had ever gone and landed way down the hill, somehow just managing to stay on my feet.

Not long after that, Arnold (a neighbour) came by to ask Dad if he would make him some skis, to which Dad agreed. About a week later, the guy came back around 8:00 p.m. on a bright moonlit evening to pick them up. Moonlight is a funny thing when there is heavy snow cover. You can see everything, but there are a few shadows in the dim moonlight, so details are obscure.

Anyway, Arnold said, "Before I take these skis, I want to try them to see if they are any good."

"Well, sir. There is a track up the hill and a good crust. Just walk up the slope 'til you see the top of the tracks and follow them down." Dad straightened his shoulders, slightly miffed. So, Arnold headed up the hill with the skis as we watched out the kitchen window.

"Harold," Mother began quizzically (and slightly concerned). "Shouldn't you have told him about the ski jump?"

"He'll find it." Dad replied smugly.

In the bright moonlight, we watched as Arnold reached the top and put on the skis. The frozen track was hard and fast. He whooshed down the hill in good form, then he hit the jump, obscured in the moonlight.

"WAAAAAAAAAAAAAAAAAAAAH!!!!"

Arnold flew in the air, pinwheeling like crazy—legs, arms, feet, and skis flailing in all four directions—then *whump!* He came down in a heap at the bottom of the hill (Figure 45).

He arose and shook himself like a large, hairy dog before retrieving the skis and heading back for the house. I don't think he even realised that there *was* a ski jump.

When he got to the house, his only comment was: "Those are some good skis. They just took right off!"

Satisfied that they worked, he left.

Figure 45. Moonlight Ski Jump

Snowshoes were a whole different level of work than skis had been. I mentioned that Dad had cut ash into three-quarter-inch square strips. The other activity (making rawhide) was less fun, and Dad started that in the fall—when he obtained a deer hide from Cousin Basil, who typically gave us a deer each year.

To make rawhide, we soaked the whole hide in a mixture of softwood ash, hardwood ash, and water…all of which we had in abundance.

The alternative is to use hydrated lime and water. We soaked the hide for about a week before stripping the hair and flesh from it. As I recall, after the soaking, Dad cut the hide into one long, continuous strip and removed the hair and flesh by pulling it over a slightly sharpened piece of angle iron. It can't be too sharp, or it will cut the hide. Pulling it also stretched the leather somewhat; that part was a slimy, stinky business.

Once the rawhide strip was clean, he stretched it again before soaking it in a baking soda and vinegar mix for a full day (to "neutralise" it). After that, he stretched it out some more then left it to dry. The rawhide was stored until he was ready to make snowshoes: When Dad would construct a design for the final shape of the snowshoe, steam the wood, and bend it around a wooden pattern before clamping it in place to dry it some more. Meanwhile, he soaked the dried rawhide to make it more flexible.

Once the snowshoe frame dried, he drilled evenly spaced holes in it for lacing and screwed together the two tail ends with a stainless-steel bolt, though a traditionalist would have lashed them together with rawhide. Dad prepared two identical snowshoe frames.

Lacing a snowshoe is an art. You'll find many how-to sites that show how this is done on the internet. I, frankly, don't know what pattern Dad used (or if he made up his own). In any event, he managed to weave the rawhide into the frame of each snowshoe. All we had to do was attach a harness to hold our boots, and away we went.

The last pair he made, I had until about 2019. He had laced them with nylon cord (which is better than rawhide because it doesn't stretch, however, it does wear out faster). Snowshoes were an essential part of getting around in the woods during the winter before snowmobiles were prevalent. They were handy in Albert County because it's so hilly, and there are thick woods. We used them *extensively* when making maple sugar or any other activity that required us to go into the woods in deep winter.

Once you got the hang of it, you could even run on them if they were balanced. You did this by attaching the snowshoe and lifting your foot. If the toe of the snowshoe tended to tilt down, you fastened a weight (typically a penny or two) to the tail of the snowshoe until the front tilted up slightly. If you tried to run and the front tilted down, you would fall flat on your face.

Imagine trying to get up when you are flat on your stomach in deep snow, with the tips of your snowshoes buried.

====

Winter Storms and Nor'easters

As sure as water freezes to ice, we were sure to lose power (and be snowed in) at least three or four times every winter. It was a fact of life in Albert County during the fifties and sixties.

All the electric wires were on hydro poles, which often would get toppled over in a severe ice storm. These storms typically blocked the roads. I remember one particularly nasty storm when Dad was late getting home. Mother worriedly checked out the window every five minutes until (at last) Dad showed up two hours late…on snowshoes, carrying his lunch pail.

"What happened?" Mother cried, rushing to help Dad off with his coat as he burst into the kitchen in a flurry of wind and snow.

Dad blew on his hands and rubbed them together. "Well, I got the car stuck on the steep hill just before the bridge and had to walk home." (This was about two miles in a raging blizzard—I told you: Snowshoes were useful!)

"What are you going to do about the car?" Mom asked.

"Not much," Dad shrugged. "I tied a rag to the antenna so the guys on the plough wouldn't hit my car. After the storm is over, I'll walk back and dig it out."

And that is precisely how it played out: The storm lasted two days, then Dad walked back to the car. As he told it, only about two feet of the antenna showed. After working three or four hours digging out the car, the guys with the plough came by to help him get it out. Then he followed them back to our place (where the snow was up to his armpits, and he had to shovel a parking spot in the driveway). Yes, I helped with the shovelling!

He ate a big supper that night.

We expected power outages and severe winter storms, so we were well prepared. We had many regular oil lamps and several Aladdin lamps. The other advantage we had was a reliance on wood-burning stoves. With a source of light, lots of wood, and a plentiful food supply, we had no problems surviving any major storm. Much later (when my parents switched to an oil furnace and stove), they always had wood as an option. In remote parts of Canada, hybrid heating systems are still standard.

Being "storm-stayed" was kind of fun—for me. With the wind howling around the house, blinding snow, and temperatures often well below zero…no one went out unless necessary. The storms typically lasted anywhere from one to three days, so we would hang out, listen to the radio, and play games in the meantime. It was fun for a kid, plus it gave the adults a chance to enjoy some downtime.

After the storm, we ventured out into a blinding white landscape. All the sharp edges were gone; a smooth, white blanket covered everything. Frequently, when we opened the back door from the woodshed, we found a drift covering the entrance and had to shovel our way out!

Winter storms varied in intensity. Ordinary winter storms came from the west and dumped a lot of snow. These were just a normal part of winter, and no one got too fussed about them. On the other hand, there were Nor'easters.

A Nor'easter is a storm that forms along the Atlantic coast of the United States and heads north, bringing high winds and rain or snow. The most feared are ice storms that can wipe out power and transportation all along the Eastern Seaboard for days—and they are *still* a problem. In 2017, a massive ice storm hit New Brunswick, and over 300,000 people lost power for several days.

In the fifties and sixties, these storms caused extensive damage, but the impact was likely less severe than today. First, we were a more rural society back then, and (as a result of that fact) more folks relied on wood heating. Second, because we were tied more closely to the land and had our pantries well stocked with our own produce, we were less dependant on supermarkets than we are today.

Ice storms were a severe threat because ice would build up on trees, telephone poles, roofs, and steel cables. At the southwest end of Baltimore is Caledonia Mountain, in the fifties, the government built a microwave transmission tower that served as a TV tower. One winter, we had a severe ice storm followed shortly after by another.

Between storms, Dad and I drove up to look (not much else to do right then), and we saw that the two-inch steel support cables were covered with at least two feet of ice and were sagging under the load. I remember Dad saying that if we had another storm or high winds, he figured the tower would come down. Sure enough, another storm arrived and down came the tower.

Ice storms made ploughing the roads difficult since the ice was tough to break up, even with a plough. These storms brought down trees, power lines, and sometimes buildings. Dad would get up on a ladder, break up the ice formed on the roof, and sometimes shovel off the roof to lighten the snow load.

On the other hand, the woods and fields were beautiful. Everything looked crystallised! The trees shimmered; the effect was dazzling when the sun came out. Wind set the trees tinkling like the largest set of wind chimes imaginable. To me, this was a magical time. My parents—who had to deal with the aftermath—found it less magical.

Nor'easters seem to be most common in early winter. By March, they tapered off, leaving us to deal with just the large dumps of heavy wet snow remaining, "heart attack snow," as Dad called it. It was hard to shovel but great for snow forts, and snowballs. At school, we made good use of it.

All in all, winter was a fun and quiet season—at least for me. The adults had more work to do…but even they had more time to snuggle in, settle down to rest, and enjoy the fruits of their year's labours before facing a new year of hard work and harvest. Even so, winter could feel long for all of us, with its heavy snow, howling storms, and reluctance to let go in spring.

When spring came to the Irving homestead, at last, the longer days and budding maples lifted everyone's spirits. We, again, had fresh produce to look forward to and the promise of warmer days ahead. It was indeed a time for renewal, in all senses of the word.

Little did we know just *how much* renewal the following spring would bring.

Part 3

Chapter 12

The Day Our House Burned Down

Any day that begins with the smell of smoke and your dad yelling "Fire!" is *not* going to be a good day.

It was a chilly Sunday morning on April 25th, 1965. Dad arose early and started the fire in the kitchen stove. About mid-morning, he went down to start a fire in the furnace...as usual for the time of year, it'd been a cold night in Baltimore (despite the warmer days), so we needed more heat. To get the furnace going more quickly, he added some large pieces of birch bark to the kindling. When his blaze was roaring away, he shut the furnace door and went back upstairs for a cup of tea—just as he had every morning for years.

Dad didn't know that on that morning, a piece of flaming birch bark had gotten sucked up the chimney and landed on dry cedar shingles. The old farmhouse not only had cedar shingles on the roof, it also had wooden clapboards on the outside and (as you'll recall, I'm sure) large sheets of birch bark that acted as a windbreak between the clapboards and the wooden frame. Fine for stopping drafts...not for stopping fires. The burning bark smouldered on the shingles for a long time—eventually, they caught fire.

Around noon, Dad smelled smoke and went outside, saw there was a fire on the roof, and raced to the attic to see if he could knock the shingles off. He tried, but it got ahead of him...even using the hose, there was no way he could stop the flames.

I was up and dressed by the time he thundered down the stairs from the attic. He ordered me to grab as many clothes as I could put in a bag and take them outside, which I did. Mother was on the phone calling the Hillsborough Fire Department. According to their records, the call came in at 12:30 p.m.

Fortunately, we had a party line—Mother could tell that someone was listening in, so she didn't have to tell anyone else. She hung up and started grabbing clothes from the upstairs bedrooms, as well as other stuff from the second floor. We carted it all out on the lawn. In about ten minutes, I had everything I wanted out of my room thrown into the yard, on a blanket. We began rescuing stuff from the other rooms. The fire was progressing by the time neighbours started to arrive.

The neighbours joined us to help with getting the fridge, washing machine, and other appliances out of the kitchen. Our old wood stove was already hot and fired up, so there was no way we were going to touch that. But we did get some of the furniture and dishes from the living room and dining room. By this point, the fire had spread too far, the roof had caved in, and we all decided there was no way we could get back into the house. I think Dad did go through a backdoor into the basement to get some equipment, but it was minor stuff. We also had the old summer kitchen, which was full of wood and attached to the house. Once the main house went up, the whole damn thing burst into a spectacular blaze.

I have vague memories of standing around with the neighbours and just watching the house burn—flames shooting from the windows as my bedroom window blew out, and then the second floor gave way. When the house collapsed on itself, we moved from the lawn to the road because the heat was so intense, and the slightest wind sent sparks and glowing embers scattering everywhere.

By the time the Hillsborough Volunteer Fire Department arrived, the house was mostly gone.[24] Roaring orange tongues of flame licked the sky, belching thick clouds of black smoke... As my Dad said later, "They arrived in time to save the basement."

The firemen poured a lot of water on it from their tanker to (eventually) put the fire out. Several people remarked that "we might have been better off just letting the whole thing finish burning" so that we wouldn't have to dig out the basement. Given the amount of work we had later, I tended to agree.

---

[24] My thanks to the Volunteers of the Hillsborough Fire Department and to my cousins, Garda and Gail, for exact times and dates.

Standing there as the house collapsed into the basement, it dawned on us: Not only were we *homeless*, we had no *insurance.*

Fortunately, we were a member of a longstanding, tight-knit community, including the people in Baltimore and the folks in Hillsborough (and surrounding areas).

Our families had lived there for several generations, and people had grown up together; known each other's families; intermarried; worked together, and attended church together. When we were burned out, the community rallied around us.

We stayed with Bea and Omer Irving for about a month. During that time, my father renovated the two-car garage that he had built across the road from the house where the old barn stood. The garage was quite large with an aluminium roof, tin sides, and three or four windows. It was just a big space. Dad built some partitions for a couple of bedrooms; plus, he installed a sink and running water. Friends and relatives donated a stove and some furniture; we also used some of the stuff we salvaged.

A month or so later, we moved into the garage (Figure 46).

Figure 46. Garage Modified for Living

It wasn't luxurious, but it was liveable. It had no insulation, and the metal roof made a racket when it rained. One vivid memory I have of living in the garage is how it sounded during a hailstorm. It was like being inside a large metal drum with an insane musician pounding away!

Though the accommodations were cold, it was tolerable because we had warm clothes and heavy flannel blankets on the beds. The kitchen stove was our only source of heat, and we kept it going nearly full tilt through May—even though it was starting to warm up outside.

Amenities were sparse. Our bathroom was an outhouse across the creek. For convenience, Dad built a rough bridge across the stream, so we didn't have to get our feet wet. Somehow, we had running water in the kitchen.

I was still in school then (finishing grade twelve), and my mother and father were *adamant* that I pay attention to my studies. Dad and Mom (with the help of neighbours) would work on the house, while I helped on weekends and after school. Eventually, we cleared out the basement. Dad and Mom got plans for a house and vigorously debated how to configure it. Finally, they settled on a floor plan. With help from neighbours and friends, Dad quickly built forms and poured the basement floor and walls, then we were ready to construct the frame.

Dad was working for TP Downey and Sons at their sawmill, where he was head of maintenance. Downey not only gave Dad time off with some pay, but they also donated lumber for our house. Other neighbours kicked in with labour and materials; and our relatives gave us some cash to help rebuild. Dad got the frame up between mid-June and had the house boxed in and roofed by mid-August.

By that time, I had graduated from high school and gone to work at the plaster mill (in Hillsborough) for the summer. Before the fire, I had been accepted at the New Brunswick Institute of Technology in their Mechanical Technology program. Again, Mother and Father insisted that I was "darn well going to go." So, rather than spend the summer helping Dad rebuild, it was off to work for me to save for college in the fall. When I had time off from the plaster mill, I worked with Dad on the house, and I *was* able to contribute financially to the family plus cover my expenses at school.

Thank God for the plaster mill! It'd been operating since 1854 and (at one time) was the largest mill of its kind in North America. It closed in 1980. Working in the mill was hard and dirty. All day, we carted fifty-pound bags of plaster into boxcars and piled them up.

I came home every night covered in plaster dust. It was hard to remove but worth it because my job paid so well.

By mid-September, Dad had the house enclosed with windows and doors, but he still had the electrical and plumbing work to do. He worked like a madman to get it done before Christmas, finishing in early December. I came home from college in Moncton on the weekends to help whenever I could.

By the time the house was ready to live in, we were pretty darn cold living in the garage. I remember some mornings I awoke to frost on the blankets! When Dad got up to make a fire in the morning, he often found the tea kettle frozen to the top of the stove. I usually got dressed under the covers, put on heavy socks and extra shirts, and (some mornings) maybe even a jacket. By 8:00 a.m. or so, the place was (if not warm, at least) bearable, and Dad would be charging off up to the house to try and get it finished.

When we finally moved into the house in December, it was habitable, but it was *not*—in any sense of the word—*finished* (Figure 47). The walls were plain insulation stapled between the joists. We had no wallboard up, just rough plywood floors and no finished ceiling, but the windows were installed and solid!

We had a stove, a functioning kitchen, an indoor bathroom, and hot water. There was a furnace in the basement, a combination of oil-fired and wood apparatus. It was heaven! Dad never used birch bark to light a fire again, from the day we moved in. And he ensured that the shingles were asphalt.

Figure 47. New House in Baltimore

Chapter 13

From Backwoods to Big City

The day you move away from home is momentous for everyone. For me, it was a gradual process of disengagement.

In the fall of 1965, I entered the Mechanical Technology program at the New Brunswick Institute of Technology (NBIT) in Moncton (as planned), boarding with my Aunt Hattie during the week. The transition to living in Moncton and attending NBIT was a *huge* change. My world had gradually expanded from a one-room country school to high school (and now) to a diploma program in the big city of Moncton.

It was my first *real* taste of a much wider world and other points of view. In school, I met students from all over New Brunswick and as far away as Kenya—the first Black person I had ever met. One fellow had been raised in a French-speaking region of northern New Brunswick, so he spoke little English. As we became friends and compared notes, we realised we were taught that the other was "not to be trusted" because of our language and religion. At that point, we both concluded that we had been taught a *load of crap*.

Living with my Aunt Hattie in Moncton during the week also expanded my horizons. She was widowed; my Uncle Charlie having died a few years previously. Having boarders helped her manage expenses, and it certainly helped me with my schooling. Living in a city and having ready access to stores, swimming, and transportation was exhilarating. Joe Cheng (from Hong Kong) was also boarding with my aunt while earning his degree, studying at the Université de Moncton. Talking with Joe (the first Asian person I had ever met), I got some insight into what life was like in Hong Kong. Joe came from a wealthy family; he was sophisticated and well travelled—at least, from my perspective.

At one point, I invited Joe and his friend down to the farm in Albert County. Both remarked that they "couldn't get over how much land we had!" Having visited Hong Kong myself now, I understand why they found it unusual.

But even as my views and horizons were expanding, my connection to home, family, and community remained strong. I lived in Moncton near the school but went home most weekends to see my family (and help my dad with the house). In June 1967, I finished my diploma program and found a job—thus, it was time to enter the wider world.

===

I Leave Home with a Crash, Not a Whimper

On July 2nd, 1967, I was scheduled to report to the Defense Research Board at Shirley's Bay in Ottawa for my first job. I was excited, and my parents were proud—if feeling a bit weepy that I was leaving. Two days before catching the train to Ottawa, I cured them of that.

It was early on a Thursday morning, I got up at 6:00 a.m. to drive Dad to work so that I could have the car to run some errands (in preparation for my big trip). Dad's car was a green VW-1500 sedan. It was built like a VW Beetle, with the engine in the rear but looked more like a conventional sedan. Anyway, off we go, I drop Dad at the mill. On the way home (eager for breakfast), I was speeding along the dirt road. All seemed well…until I headed down a steep hill a bit faster than usual and hit some washboard ruts in the dirt road. Well damn! The car started swerving from side to side, and when I hit the brakes, it flipped over entirely. I remember that time seemed to stop as the car rolled upside down into the ditch. I fell into the upside-down roof before crawling out.

I wasn't hurt much except for a bruised knee—not bad for lacking seatbelts.[25]

---

[25] They weren't mandatory in New Brunswick until 1983.

Fortunately, a neighbour was passing by and stopped: "Havin' a problem?"

"Yup, I flipped the car."

"Well, let's find your dad and see what we can do about it. Don't feel too bad. Driving one of them rear-engine cars is like trying to throw a dart backwards, and I bet your dad would have rolled it sooner or later."

That helped, but I was worried about Dad's reaction.

All in all, he took it well. He just wanted to know I was all right. Then, he wanted to see the car. So, off we went, back to the accident. Using a tow rope, we righted the car (which hadn't suffered much damage). I hadn't been going *that* fast. There were some dents and scrapes. The worst damage was to the upholstery in the roof, as battery acid leaked onto it. Anyway, we got the car started and drove home. Oddly, Mom and Dad seemed less distraught at my leaving after that.

Chapter 14

Reflections

Subsequently, I earned three degrees, travelled the world, lived in two other countries for extended periods and became a tenured professor—but those are stories for another time. But for all my education and world travels, I learned my most important lessons right there in tiny Baltimore, New Brunswick.

Watching our house burn to ashes in 1965, I learned the importance of community and the unimportance of things. We had no fire insurance, and (though my dad made a reasonable salary) we had no vast cash reserves. We did have family, friends, and good neighbours. A tight-knit community! The neighbours rallied around with goods, clothing, furniture, food, or whatever we needed until we got back on our feet. If not for the generosity of the local community, we would have been in desperate circumstances. We were not unique, as others with similar experiences had similar outcomes.

Tight-knit communities have downsides, but they have many upsides as well. For example, when I organised my parents' fiftieth wedding anniversary, we held it at the church in Hillsborough (with locals providing food, music, and "entertainment"). Clyde Downey (the owner of the mill where Dad worked), some of his family, and about thirty local folks (of all socioeconomic levels) attended the event. It was a community affair!

Watching our house disintegrate into ash taught me that the loss of things isn't important; it is losing the memories they evoke. When I pick up an old book or a teacup, its value to me is in the associations, not the thing itself. We lost the house; we rebuilt the house. But, much of our family history was lost in the ashes—all we retained were the memories; and in the end, that's all anyone has.

Reconstructing and preserving memories is one motivation for writing this book. The other reason was to reflect on how technology changed and how that change affected our lives.

As you will recall, my mother and father came from large families. This was a combination of a lack of access to birth control technology and the need for large families to work the farm. As technology improved for both birth control and farming, families grew smaller. One effect for me was that I knew many only children. Smaller families meant less expense and fewer offspring to look after ageing parents—something that I experienced directly.

The other main changes were improved transportation and electrification. In 1947, I was born into a home without electricity, running water or indoor plumbing. By 1967, these amenities were common. Better sanitation led to better health. Access to reliable electricity led to televisions, refrigerators, and other electrical appliances.

In 1967, homes in Baltimore looked much like they would today—except for computers, cell phones, and the internet. Phones were less costly, and ground transportation became easier—roads were being paved and ploughed regularly—many fewer snow days at home.

Improvements to the provincial transportation grid meant fewer small grocery stores and the beginning of the "supermarkets" we know today. They often had a selection of imported products in winter, and advances in refrigeration technology resulted in a wide variety of frozen food becoming available.

Many relied on their gardens for vegetables (some still canned or froze their food), but many relied on the supermarket. We were becoming more sophisticated but less independent. New Brunswick still saw a net outflow of young people (and others) looking for work. Jobs in the traditional logging, fishing, and mining industries were becoming highly mechanised, and there were fewer (though usually better) jobs available as a result. I was just one of many who was "Goin' Down the Road," as they'd say![26]

The outflow of people stripped communities of their future, as

---

[26] *Goin' Down the Road* was a 1970 film about two friends who left Nova Scotia for Toronto.

the youth left for jobs out of the province. All was not lost, however, because improved roads meant that many people who worked in the city could live further afield. So, outsiders moved into rural communities. Many integrated well...but for others, the isolation and trials of rural life (with swarms of bugs in summer and tons of snow in winter) proved too much. They left, to be replaced by others.

This turbulence changed the nature of relationships. Formerly, people formed close bonds and were willing to invest in relationships; because the community was stable. However, with much greater mobility, how much will you commit to a relationship with a neighbour if they are likely to move next year? This change is still working itself out, fifty years later.

Ironically, we may see a reversal of this outflow in 2021 (due to Covid-19 and technology). People working at home due to Covid-19 are now asking themselves: "Why not move to the country where I can afford a lovely property? If I have access to reliable Wi-Fi, I can work anywhere!"

There is an inflow of people from Ontario to the Maritimes seeking a cheaper, more laid-back lifestyle. Who knows where that will lead?

In closing, here are a few other things I learned.

As I mentioned earlier (regarding our house burning down), there is tremendous value in a connected and supportive community. Individuals have a sense of belonging, and with belonging comes respect for property and each other. I noticed this twenty years later when I lived in a not-for-profit housing co-operative in Toronto. Because the building residents worked on various boards and committees to run the building, they got to know each other.

Because we knew each other, we built a small, vertical community in the heart of downtown Toronto. These interpersonal connections had direct economic implications; since the cost-per-square-foot of maintaining a not-for-profit co-op apartment building was *much lower* than for public housing. It was their home and community; people felt responsible for maintaining it.

From both my parents, I learned to take personal responsibility for my actions and step up to help solve a problem.

Dealing with my dog was a harsh but necessary lesson in this regard—but there were many others. I never saw my mother or father dodge their responsibilities or a hard decision.

From Dad, I learned to treat life's difficulties as "problems to be dealt with and solved." Whether it be freeing a truck stuck in the mud or dynamiting bedrock for a septic tank, he was always thoughtful, careful, and analytic.

From Mother, I learned the power of hard work, modesty, kindness, and the strength of quiet convictions.

Ultimately, the most important lesson I learned was the simplest: Things change.

If life is going badly, don't do anything irrevocable because…things change.

If everything is going well, don't get overconfident because…things change.

When you have trouble, don't be a whiner, deal with it, because…things change.

And if you are on top of the world, don't be an arrogant ass because…

THINGS CHANGE!

About the Author

Richard (Rick) Irving, D.Tech., B.A.Sc., MASc., Ph.D., is uniquely qualified to write this book. He grew up in the fifties and sixties in rural New Brunswick, Canada; went to one-room country schools; and ultimately completed a Ph.D. at the University of Waterloo. Eventually, he had a thirty-five-year career as a tenured professor at the Schulich School of Business at York University in Toronto. On the way, he had three marriages, travelled the world , taught on four continents, lived in New York for two years, and spent a year in Provence before it was fashionable. Rick was in Lisbon in April 1974 during the Carnation Revolution ; he was once detained by the police in southern France for hitchhiking; he hiked part of the Inca Trail; and he was briefly barred from a Toys "R" Us.

Over a forty-year career, he specialized in studying how organizations adapt to changes in technology. Rick has published fourteen academic articles, numerous reports, and two books—*Office Information Systems: Management Issues and Methods*, Wiley, 1991, and *Don't Leave IT to the Geeks*, Pheasant Ridge, 2001.

Rick was president and CEO of Hazelburn Co-op, a non-profit housing co-op; president of Beatty Buddies, a non-profit daycare; and past president and ex-member of the board of HIMSS Ontario, a non-profit Association for IT Healthcare Professionals. He was a contributing editor for Canadian Healthcare Technology, writing a regular column on Healthcare and IT, from 2000 to 2014, when he retired from that position.

Currently, he is enjoying retirement and is active in his Port Credit community.